RAISING THE PERFECTLY IMPERFECT CHILD

Facing Challenges with
Strength, Courage, and Hope

BORIS VUJICIC

FOREWORD BY NICK VUJICIC

WATERBROOK
PRESS

RAISING THE PERFECTLY IMPERFECT CHILD
PUBLISHED BY WATERBROOK PRESS
12265 Oracle Boulevard, Suite 200
Colorado Springs, Colorado 80921

This book is not intended to replace the medical advice of a trained medical professional. Readers are advised to consult a physician or other qualified health-care professional regarding treatment of their medical problems. The author and publisher specifically disclaim liability, loss, or risk, personal or otherwise, which is incurred as a consequence, directly or indirectly, of the use or application of any of the contents of this book.

Scripture quotations or paraphrases are taken from the following versions: The ESV® Bible (the Holy Bible, English Standard Version®), copyright © 2001 by Crossway, a publishing ministry of Good News Publishers. Used by permission. All rights reserved. The Holy Bible, New International Version®, NIV®. Copyright © 1973, 1978, 1984, 2011 by Biblica Inc.® Used by permission. All rights reserved worldwide. The New King James Version®. Copyright © 1982 by Thomas Nelson Inc. Used by permission. All rights reserved. The Holy Bible, New Living Translation, copyright © 1996, 2004, 2007, 2013 by Tyndale House Foundation. Used by permission of Tyndale House Publishers Inc., Carol Stream, Illinois 60188. All rights reserved.

Hardcover ISBN 978-1-60142-834-9
eBook ISBN 978-1-60142-836-3

Cover design by Kristopher K. Orr; cover and insert photos courtesy of the Vujicic family

Published in the United States by WaterBrook Multnomah, an imprint of the Crown Publishing Group, a division of Penguin Random House LLC, New York.

WATERBROOK® and its deer colophon are registered trademarks of Penguin Random House LLC.

Library of Congress Cataloging-in-Publication Data
Names: Vujicic, Boris.
Title: Raising the perfectly imperfect child : facing challenges with strength, courage, and hope / Boris Vujicic.
Description: First Edition. | Colorado Springs, Colorado : WaterBrook Press, 2016.
Identifiers: LCCN 2015036781| ISBN 9781601428349 | ISBN 9781601428363 (electronic)
Subjects: LCSH: Parents of children with disabilities—Religious life. | Parenting—Religious aspects—
  Christianity. | Child rearing—Religious aspects—Christianity. | Children with disabilities—Care. |
  Vujicic, Nick.
Classification: LCC BV4596.P35 V85 2016 | DDC 248.8/45—dc23
LC record available at http://lccn.loc.gov/2015036781

Printed in the United States of America
2016—First Edition

10 9 8 7 6 5 4 3 2 1

SPECIAL SALES
Most WaterBrook Multnomah books are available at special quantity discounts when purchased in bulk by corporations, organizations, and special-interest groups. Custom imprinting or excerpting can also be done to fit special needs. For information, please e-mail SpecialMarkets@WaterBrookMultnomah.com or call 1-800-603-7051.

This book is dedicated to all those who have helped my
wife and me to encourage and support Nick over the years,
especially to our other children, Aaron and Michelle,
as well as to our daughter-in-law Kanae, our parents
and family members, and, of course, God,
our primary Source of strength through Christ Jesus.

Contents

Foreword by Nick Vujicic

I was born without limbs, and my disabilities have brought many challenges, yet I've often said anyone who grows up without loving and supportive parents has far more to overcome than I did. I can't imagine how difficult that would be.

My father and mother were always there for me. That's not to say they coddled me or gave me everything I wanted. As my father notes in this wise and insightful book, my grandparents and others often wondered how my mother could not rush to help me as I struggled to stand as a toddler.

"Let him figure it out," my mum would say. "He needs to do things for himself."

I admit this approach sometimes annoyed me, especially when my parents required me to earn my allowance by vacuuming the house, cleaning my room, and making my bed. Then there were the many long nights Dad drilled me on math problems while my idle Nintendo games called me to come play.

I understand now that they were being good parents. They worked to instill a strong work ethic, personal responsibility, and a foundation of faith in me and in my brother and sister as well. They also told me nearly every day that there were no limits on my life. "You may lack limbs, but you can do anything you want," they said.

Later my father and mother may have wondered if they were too successful at giving me the roots and wings to become an independent adult. At the age of nineteen, I announced plans for my first international speaking tour. I had arranged to travel to South Africa with the goal of giving away twenty thousand dollars in savings to needy orphans there.

My parents strongly objected to this audacious plan, as you might imagine. They were concerned for my safety while journeying through a rugged part of the world in a wheelchair. And they were shocked that I would dish out my hard-earned nest egg at such a young age.

I reminded them that they'd always said there were no limits on my life, and every single night of my childhood they'd made sure I prayed and asked God to help the poor children of the world.

"You planted the seeds for this!" I said.

They were not amused, but they did not stand in my way. Mum and Dad are still sometimes taken aback by my big dreams and adventurous spirit, but they are always encouraging and willing to pitch in.

They are not perfect, of course, but to borrow from this book's title, they are "perfectly imperfect." The older I get, the more I realize the parental warnings and rules that bothered me in my teen years were actually signs of a caring mother and father preparing me for a productive and accomplished life.

Still, it is a little disconcerting to consider that my father has been proven right about nearly everything he cautioned me against, warned me to avoid, or emphatically told me not to do! There were so many times I thought he was dead wrong, but as it turned out, he was usually dead right.

My father always seems to be three steps ahead of me. I have this nagging feeling I will never catch up. Sometimes as a child I wondered if there was more than one of him or if he had superpowers. He juggled three jobs, started several churches as a lay pastor, and helped my working mum do all it took to raise a disabled daredevil and two other lively kids.

Yet whenever we needed Dad, he miraculously appeared.

This occurred on the night after I'd tried to drown myself in the bathtub and then told my little brother my plan to commit suicide before the age of twenty-one. My parents didn't know about the suicide attempt, and neither did my brother. But Aaron went to Dad and told him what I'd said about killing myself before I turned twenty-one.

My father came to my room and talked calmly to me. He offered assurance that mum and he loved me, that my brother and sister loved me, and that God loved me too.

Then my dad sat on my bed and gently stroked my hair until I fell asleep. I will never forget that.

Oh, we do still bang heads because we are so much alike. We have the same intense drive and strong-willed temperament. He predicted that I will probably butt heads with my kids too. When we announced that Kanae was pregnant with our first child, he smiled and said, "Now you'll see what it's like to be a father."

Once again, Dad was spot on. I tell my son Kiyoshi to pick up his toys. I will one day make him do chores to earn his allowance. Already at night, I remind him to pray and ask God to help the poor children around the world. Then I put my chin on his head and nuzzle him until he falls asleep. I hope he never forgets that.

Perfectly imperfect sons become perfectly imperfect fathers. I pray that I'm as good a parent as my mother and father. Still, I can think of one thing I will do differently with my son. When Kiyoshi comes to me at the age of nineteen and announces that he's traveling to some faraway place to give all his savings to the orphans, I will say, "I'm coming with you!"

Thanks for everything, Mom and Dad. You prepared me for a ridiculously good life. You encouraged me to pursue a life without limits, and you showed me how to love without limits.

Kanae and I will do the same for our children.

Love,

Nick

One

The Perfectly Imperfect Child

Accept, Love, and Learn from Your Unique Child

My wife, Dushka, and I were excited and more than a little nervous. The prenatal tests had looked fine for the baby. There'd been no problems at all during this pregnancy. When the baby made it known that he was ready, my wife went to the delivery room with the doctor and nurses. I prayed while waiting for the call to join her, adding to the hundreds of prayers I'd offered up in the preceding months.

Dushka was a nurse and a midwife. She and I were well aware of the potential for problems in a pregnancy and during the delivery. So many things can go wrong. I'd often thought a normal birth is a miracle.

Since this was a first pregnancy, we knew the delivery might take a long time, and it did. Twelve hours of labor passed before the call came and I was allowed into the room. The first thing that struck me was the joy in my wife's eyes. I shared her elation when I looked to the tiny form resting upon his mother's chest: a baby boy with two arms, two legs, and a beautiful face.

He was a perfectly formed, beautiful child of God.

Our first grandchild!

My beaming son, Nick, the proud father, was at the bedside of his wife, Kanae, the mother. It was a miracle! Nick was euphoric, so happy he seemed to levitate over his wife and newborn son, nuzzling them, kissing them, reassuring himself they were real—his own family at last.

This was a moment Nick, Dushka, and I had hardly dared to dream about. We'd feared that because he had been born with neither arms nor legs, Nick would never find a wife or have a family. But within two short years, what had seemed impossible had become a reality. Nick had met and won the heart of a beautiful, soulful, and spiritual young Christian woman, Kanae Miyahara.

One year and one day after their marriage, their son Kiyoshi was born.

TAKEN BY SURPRISE

Seven months earlier, Kanae and Nick had done their best to make the surprise announcement of her pregnancy memorable—and they certainly succeeded. We gathered at Nick and Kanae's home for a belated Father's Day party because Nick had been traveling. Our daughter, Michelle, was visiting, so she joined us for a wonderful dinner prepared by Kanae. After the main course, Kanae brought out a cake for dessert. We wondered at first if she'd lost her usual graceful touch as a decorator. Half of it was covered in blue icing. The other half was pink. We were clueless about the purpose of this color scheme. We took the cake but not the hint.

I didn't even catch on to her little secret when Kanae asked, "Okay, Dad, do you want a blue slice or a pink slice?"

"Blue," I said.

Dushka didn't pick up on the hints either. In fact she didn't want any cake at all.

I'd already started eating my blue cake when Kanae said with a laugh, "Well, obviously my hints didn't work for you."

I was way behind the learning curve as usual, but Dushka and Michelle screamed out, "You're pregnant!"

The not-so-subtle symbolism of the blue-and-pink cake finally became clear to dull-headed Dad. I joined in the celebration of Father's Day—the first time I had shared the holiday's guest-of-honor role with my son, the father-to-be.

Our first Father's Day together was truly one of the highlights of my life, and it was made all the sweeter by the emotional journey we had traveled with Nick through his childhood and into manhood. We'd had no idea that Nick would be born without limbs, and though doctors reassured our family time and again that it was not an inherited trait, we certainly were relieved when Kiyoshi was born with all the standard-issue appendages.

The arrival of our grandson washed away any lingering pain from the grief and fear we experienced when his father was born. Such a contrast between those two events in our lives. Such relief that God had a different plan for our grandson.

Yet by the time Kiyoshi was born, I'd come to have a much different view of what constitutes a perfectly made human being. My wife and I were life-long Christians, yet we had each experienced a crisis of faith when Nick was born. We could not believe that a loving God would burden us with such a severely disabled child. Was He punishing us for reasons neither of us could fathom?

We would come to realize our reaction was very typical for the parents of a disabled child, but at the time we lacked perspective. We also lacked the power to look into the future and see what was in store for Nick, who eventually proved to be an incredible blessing, not only to our family, but also to millions around the world.

WONDERFULLY MADE

With our limited vision, Dushka and I could foresee only struggle and anguish for Nick and for us. We were so wrong, of course. Our son and our experiences with him have enriched our lives beyond measure and taught us many lessons at the heart of this book. Nick gave us a new definition of the ideal child and a deeper appreciation for the complexity of our Father's divine vision.

Nick taught us to find new meaning in the psalm that says we are "wonderfully made." We came to see Nick as God's beautiful creation, lovingly formed in His image. We lacked the wisdom, initially, to understand that. We saw Nick as disabled rather than enabled. We could not grasp that his missing arms and legs were part of God's unique plan for our son.

When people around the world see Nick, they understand immediately that he had to overcome substantial physical and emotional challenges. They can imagine what it must have taken to build such a positive and remarkable life as a speaker and evangelist who travels the world helping others and giving hope to all. For that reason, when Nick speaks to them with messages of inspiration and faith, they are moved and impacted in profound and life-changing ways.

Dushka and I know now that Nick and Kiyoshi and all children are perfectly formed. It took us a long time to attain that knowledge. We went through many difficult days and nights to reach that enlightenment. The low points were deep. Yet all the pain and frustration we endured while parenting our remarkable son has only made his victories and achievements all the sweeter and more meaningful.

TWO VERY DIFFERENT BIRTHS

The arrival of a first grandchild is a special moment for every grandparent. When I saw Nick place his forehead to that of his newborn son and nuzzle him for the first time, my soul soared. Nick's birth was such a shock and so frightening. Kiyoshi's was just the opposite—an incredibly blissful experience.

Kiyoshi was born with a normal body and thus seemed perfect to all who viewed him. Yet just as we had no vision of the life Nick would create, we cannot foresee what God has in mind for our grandson. Will our "perfect" grandson be able to follow and surpass the achievements of his "imperfect" father? There are some big shoes to fill, but I don't think that is really important. I want Kiyoshi to be happy and fulfilled according to his own desires and expectations.

What is important, I believe, is that we place no limits on our children. We should not burden them with our expectations, because our vision is no match for that of our Creator. There is a tendency to think a glass can be either half empty or half full, but there is a third option—the glass is always full. It may not be full of a liquid, but what is not liquid is oxygen. We usually measure only what we can see. The truth of things is often hidden from us, like the invisible oxygen that fills the glass.

When Nick was born, his path in life seemed very steep. We failed to account for the human capacity to rise above and soar beyond. Beethoven gradually lost his hearing during the last twenty-five years of his life when he composed some of his most renowned symphonies.

He was disabled as far as his hearing, but he didn't write from what he heard; he created music from the heart. Stephen Hawking has thrived in a forty-year career as a theoretical physicist and author despite being severely disabled and, eventually, paralyzed by motor neuron disease. In effect he has no arms, no legs, and only a shell of a body. Heart is what really matters. The strength of our spirits can overcome nearly any weakness of the body.

Over time our son revealed to us what we could not see when we looked at that limbless cherub in the maternity ward. He humbled us and forced us to open our eyes and our minds. Nick seemed incomplete at birth, but it was our perception that was flawed.

FEAR VERSUS FAITH

After Nick was born, Dushka and I had great trepidation—not only about his limitations, but also about our own. We did not feel at all capable of providing for the basic needs of such a child, let alone raising him to be a happy, self-confident, and high-achieving adult.

Certainly we have not been perfect parents to Nick or to our other two children, Michelle and Aaron. Dushka and I have our strengths, in particular our shared faith, but we were tested in every possible way while raising Nick. The strength of our love for each other was tested many times, sometimes nearly to the breaking point.

Yet, with God's help, we brought Nick to adulthood. I'd like to say we molded him into the man he is today. The truth is probably more that we succeeded in not ruining the man God created Nick to be. I readily admit, for example, that Nick found his purpose as an inspirational speaker and evangelist without any guidance or even much support from me. I didn't see that potential in him, but I didn't try to stop him once he believed it was possible. I'm very grateful for that.

I did suggest that he should have a backup plan, however, and I pretty much insisted that he get the education necessary to support that backup plan if he needed it. Nick didn't thank me then, but he does now. I did it out of love, of course, and because it was our parental responsibility to guide Nick, sometimes blindly, sometimes with purpose.

We began our journey with Nick with a very narrow focus on what he lacked. Over time, though, that view changed because Nick seemed to find ways to do whatever he needed to do or figured it out with help from us. Gradually our focus shifted away from what Nick could not do to what he could do. That simple shift in focus made a big difference in our feelings and our daily approach to parenting.

Many parents whose children have severe disabilities seek us out when we attend events with Nick. Others write or e-mail us. Most of them give me more inspiration than I could hope to provide them. Still, just knowing that you are not alone and that others share your feelings and fears can bring solace and comfort. I am grateful for the opportunity to help other parents in any way possible. In that regard, being Nick's father has brought many great rewards.

BLESSED TO SHARE

In the spring of 2014, Dushka and I journeyed to Vietnam to attend a stadium event featuring Nick, who by that time was an internationally known best-selling author, inspirational speaker, and evangelist. With more than 7.5 million followers on Facebook, 350,000 on Twitter, and at least twenty-nine YouTube videos, many with one to four million views each, Nick has become one of the world's most well-known and beloved disabled individuals.

Because of Nick, the parents of other disabled and special-needs children are drawn to us. They know we have been through what they are experiencing and have many questions, just as we did. When we began our journey with Nick, these questions kept us awake and trembling at night:

- How will we keep this child alive?
- Will he be able to feed or dress himself one day?
- Is his mind damaged too?
- How will we educate him?
- Will our child ever have a normal life?
- How can we help him be self-sufficient?
- If we have other children, will they have the same challenges?
- How do we explain his disabilities to him? To siblings? To other children?

- How do we teach a child with so many challenges to love God and to know God loves him?
- How do we give this child hope and a strong spirit?
- How will we ever have the strength and resources we need to guide this child?

Dushka and I are humbled and often brought to tears by the stories told to us by other parents. Mostly, though, we are grateful for the opportunity to provide them with hope, as well as a model for raising a physically disabled child into an accomplished and well-balanced adult.

Nick often says that while he has never received the miracle he sought as a boy—to be made whole with arms and legs—God has put him in a position to serve as a miracle to others, to offer them inspiration and to encourage them in faith. My wife and I have been blessed in much the same way. We prayed for limbs on Nick's behalf after his birth and for many years afterward. As you can imagine, we also prayed for wisdom, or at least someone to guide us in our efforts to parent a child facing a daunting future.

During Nick's childhood, we never found other parents who'd raised a limbless child from birth, so the help and insight we sought did not come. We had to figure it out ourselves through many trials and errors. Therefore, we are grateful to be able to give parents with disabled children encouragement, guidance, and practical advice based on our own journey.

BLESSINGS BEYOND BELIEF

I reflected on that journey during our trip to Vietnam with Nick. In this country so different from any I'd ever known, I felt peace and gratitude as thousands of people cheered for their hero, our son. Dushka and I watched in wonder as members of the audience jockeyed for positions to take his photograph, to speak with him, to touch or hug him.

For years after Nick was born, Dushka and I had allowed ourselves little hope for his future. I could not fathom that he would grow into such a strong and accomplished man, let alone a husband and father. Nick is proof that none of us are limited by our circumstances and that all of us can create meaningful, fulfilling, and joyful lives if we choose to focus on our gifts rather than on what we may lack. All of us are imperfect. All of us are perfect.

My son has written about those themes in his books, which have sold successfully around the world. My approach for this book is from a different perspective—a parent's. My wife and I would never claim any special gifts for parenting. We were ill prepared in almost every way possible when Nick came along. We are both from immigrant families who fled religious persecution, so we do have some resilience and inner strength in our heritage. Nick's success as an adult, however, is all the work of our truly remarkable son and God's incredible power. How wrong can a parent be? Well, it turns out I can be incredibly wrong, and this is true for all parents. We can all be blind to the potential of our children, even those kids born without disabilities. I have always considered myself a man of strong faith. I've served as a lay pastor and established churches. Yet when my son was born without limbs, I did not trust that God had a plan for him, one that would far surpass anything my wife and I could imagine.

Nick showed us the way. Even as a toddler, he taught us that his value and potential were beyond the reach of our limited vision. Our son is proof that through faith and determination, all things are possible. And Nick is not alone in proving this point.

As we observed on that trip to Vietnam and on many others with our son, Nick is a magnet for other disabled people. We've been overwhelmed and inspired by men, women, and children who have overcome incredible mental, emotional, and physical challenges to rise above and live beyond their limitations and circumstances.

Though my wife and I once wondered if God was punishing us by giving us a child with no limbs, we have come to realize what a gift he is to us and to the world. Indeed, because of Nick we know for certain that Scripture is correct when it tells us that "all things are possible to him who believes." More than ever we understand that what is impossible to men is possible to God.

Where once we were devastated, Dushka and I are now proud and honored to be the parents of Nick. We are thankful that God used us as guides and supporters for such a courageous, resilient, faithful, and loving person. Our greatest gift through Nick, beyond any other—except maybe our grandsons, Kiyoshi and Dejan—has been the honor of serving as sources of hope, inspiration, and guidance to other parents of disabled children.

This book is meant to be useful for all parents who feel overwhelmed or underequipped, and especially those mothers and fathers who have special-needs or disabled children. The primary goal is to light a path to a brighter tomorrow so that you, in turn, can guide your child to make the most of life.

I encourage all parents to reject labels and to look instead into the hearts of their children. Teachers, physicians, and psychologists put labels on kids because that is what they know, but they don't know what is inside the individual they have categorized as a slow learner, dyslexic, Down syndrome, disabled, or special needs.

We always fought any attempt to label or marginalize Nick because we wanted our bright and unstoppable son to have every opportunity to prove his value in the world. Subjective assessments, perceptions, and prejudices are illusory. All children have strengths and weaknesses, and they can surprise you in so many ways. Our duty is to nurture, encourage, and motivate them, and help them build upon their strengths.

Dushka and I know what it is like to carry the constant weight of guilt, frustration, and uncertainty that can accompany the birth of a child with special needs and disabilities. Our experiences with Nick taught us patience, flexibility, perseverance, and a depth of faith we'd never known before.

TEACHING BY EXAMPLE

Another important point I want to make is that the key to raising any child into a successful adult is to provide that child with a role model for success. As the classic Edgar Guest poem says, "There are little eyes upon you, and they're watching night and day." How you live is far more important than anything you say to your child. Children are very observant and will call you out anytime your actions do not match your words.

All children are ideally made for the lives God intended and created for them. Sin and evil can thwart the plans of God, so it is up to us to help our children find and fulfill those plans. The guidance provided in this book will include and build upon what Dushka and I have learned and shared along the way in these specific areas:

- Understanding that all God's children are perfectly made, and maintaining a positive and proactive approach to parenting special-needs and disabled children.
- Allowing yourself to grieve without guilt upon learning of your child's disability.
- Moving toward acceptance and adjusting expectations without losing heart or hope despite dealing with the additional stress and costs of raising a special-needs child.
- Keeping an open mind, listening, and observing so that your child can teach you how to be the best possible parent.
- Learning to be your child's best medical advocate and knowing the right questions to ask of professionals.

- Making sure all your children receive the love and attention they need and deserve, because the siblings of special-needs kids often feel neglected, guilty, or obligated to be "superkids" for their overburdened parents.
- Choosing the best methods for educating your child and then dealing with the challenges that will come with any system or bureaucracy.
- Preparing your child for the world while also preparing yourself to let go, which includes building a strong emotional foundation for dealing with insecurities and bullying and which allows your child to make mistakes and experience failure in order to grow into the most self-sufficient and productive adult possible.
- Maximizing communication, seeking understanding, and spending time together as a couple and as a family to support each other and to nurture and love your child.
- Leaning on your faith. We have experienced the power of prayer in our marriage, and every couple parenting a child should feel free to ask for spiritual guidance and help.

Wherever Nick goes, his fans and supporters line up for hours to meet and hug him. In some cities, they've had to close down streets because so many want to just see him. We are often asked how we raised him to be such an optimistic, determined, accomplished, and faith-filled man despite the challenges of his disabilities. This book is my answer to that question.

After God, Nick deserves most of the credit. My son's approach to life offers strong testimony to the power of faith and the human spirit. When your child is old enough to read and comprehend, I encourage you to introduce him or her to Nick's videos and books. Let your child see that someone born with an imperfect body can grow into a man with a perfect purpose, a man who lives, as he says, "a ridiculously good life."

TAKEAWAY THOUGHTS

- Your child's disability does not define the person he or she will become.
- Your first perceptions about raising your child will not be your reality. With time, the reality is often much more rewarding than you'd thought.
- Often what seems at first like a great burden proves to be an incredible gift.
- Know that many other parents have gone through this. Seek their advice and counsel at every opportunity.
- You know only what you have experienced in the past; embrace what you are about to learn.
- Have faith that you will find the strength and support you need if you remain open to them.

Two

A Shocking Birth

Give Yourself Permission to Grieve and Time to Recover

No couple expects that unrelenting grief will be their most prominent emotion upon the birth of their first child. I feel uncomfortable even expressing that in print, especially because our son eventually brought so much joy into our lives and to millions of people around the world.

Still, I want other parents of disabled and special-needs children to know grief is a common and understandable reaction initially. Eventually I realized my sorrow wasn't so much over Nick being born as an "imperfect" child; it was more due to the loss of the "perfect" child we had been expecting.

Many parents have told me they went through very similar experiences, and all of them, like me, felt guilty and confused by that reaction. I learned to forgive myself for these thoughts and feelings, and I encourage others to do the same. We are all human. Few of us have the strength of the Bible's Job.

Dushka, who was then twenty-five years old, went in for her final ultrasound examination eight weeks before Nick was born. During the procedure, the technician told her that our child was definitely a boy. The tech pointed to the screen on her ultrasound machine and said, "Look, it's easy to determine the sex on your baby because his legs are not in the way."

At the time her comment seemed normal and did not raise any concerns, but her words would become haunting in recollection. Dushka did question her doctor during her pregnancy because she thought the baby seemed a bit undersized and situated low in the womb. He assured us that everything seemed normal.

We had no reason to doubt the medical professionals because Dushka was one herself, and she respected their opinions. She'd also taken every precaution during her pregnancy. She had never been a smoker, and she did not consume any alcohol or take any medications during pregnancy.

When Dushka went into labor, she refused painkillers. Everything went as expected initially. I was in the birthing suite with her and the doctor and nurses. There was a tense moment early on when the midwife found that the baby was in the brow position, which means the head and neck are slightly extended so that the largest area of the head has to fit through the pelvis during delivery. Often a baby will tuck its chin as delivery begins, which is the desired position, but if the child remains in the brow position, doctors will do a safer Caesarean delivery.

We were relieved when the midwife later found that our baby had moved his head into the more desirable position. At that point, I was also extremely happy I had talked Dushka out of her desire to have our first baby at home with me assisting in the delivery under her guidance. I would not have wanted to be responsible for handling a complication in the delivery process without a full medical team and a hospital's resources.

As it turned out my relief was short lived. The delivery room doctor used forceps to pull Nick through the birth canal. His head and neck came out, and then right away I noticed our son's right shoulder looked unusual. The shoulder first appeared to be unusually shaped, and then I saw that there appeared to be no arm.

It was difficult to tell for sure from my poor vantage point. The medical team moved in and blocked my view, so I had only a brief look at that one part of our baby's body before they moved him to a far corner of the room for further examination. They said nothing.

I didn't want to believe what I'd seen. All the air seemed to drain from my lungs. Dushka had not seen our baby yet. Her view was blocked too. After delivery, she expected the delivery-room nurse to return quickly with the baby and place him on her chest, which was the standard routine. When that did not happen, Dushka grew concerned.

"Is the baby okay?" she asked.

I still hear her trembling voice in my dreams. The question was met with silence. The doctor and nursing staff were huddled around our child in a corner of the room. Dushka asked again, her tone more urgent. Again there was no response.

My mind was frantically trying to process what I thought I'd seen during the delivery. It had happened so quickly. I questioned whether I'd really seen a shoulder with no arm. When the medical team refused to respond to Dushka, I felt queasy and clutched my stomach. A staff member observed this and escorted me outside without a word.

As I left the delivery room, I heard a strange word uttered by one of the nurses: *phocomelia*. I had no idea what it meant, but it terrified me. I sat down on a chair in the courtyard with my hands covering my face. I didn't know what was going on, but I could sense something was terribly wrong.

It seemed like a long time before the pediatrician came out. He told me that Dushka had been sedated and was resting.

"I need to talk to you about your baby," he said.

I interrupted his next words, saying, "He's got no arm."

"Your child has no arms or legs," the doctor said.

"What? No arms and no legs at all?"

He nodded grimly to affirm. Later he explained that *phocomelia* is the medical term for missing or severely malformed limbs. I've never been punched hard in the head, but I imagine the jolt to your brain would be similar to how I felt in that moment. My first thought was to get to Dushka before anyone else told her. I rose, and the pediatrician put a comforting hand on my shoulder as we returned to the birthing suite. My brain was racing, yet my body felt numb, my bones hollow, and my veins empty of blood.

I tried to think of how I could break this stunning news to my wife, but when I stepped into the room, the sound of her weeping made it clear that someone had already told her. I was not happy about that. I wanted to be there to support and comfort her when she learned. It was too late. I leaned down and held her, caressing her back and shoulders, trying to absorb her pain and ease her anguish. Her body convulsed with sobs, and I soon joined her.

Dushka was still groggy from her long labor and the sedation; after a few minutes she went silent, and I realized she was asleep. I left her, hoping she would rest and regain strength before awakening to the difficult decisions that awaited us.

While Dushka slept, I went to the nursery and observed my son up close for the first time. He was among a group of newborns wrapped in their blankets. He was sleeping and looked very cute, a typically adorable newborn, so innocent and so unaware there was anything at all different about him.

A nurse brought Nick to me, and I held him for the first time. I was surprised that he felt like such a substantial child, very solid and strong. He weighed about six pounds, and his sturdiness surprised and comforted me. He seemed like a normal, lovable child.

Holding him stirred up conflicting emotions. I ached to love him. I could sense a connection growing, yet I had so many fears and doubts: *Am I strong enough to raise such a child? What sort of life can we give him? Will he need more than we can provide?*

The nurse offered to help me remove the blanket around Nick. I wasn't sure if I was ready to see his body, but I agreed. As you might imagine, I was overwhelmed to see my son's sweet baby face and then his tiny trunk bereft of arms or legs. Oddly enough, his torso seemed quite streamlined and even beautifully formed because the arm and leg sockets were covered in smooth, soft flesh.

The most striking differences on further inspection were the rudimentary "feet" attached to his little body. On his right side, there was what appeared to be a small, undeveloped foot. A more fully formed foot, with two distinct toes seemingly fused together, was attached to the bottom left side of his torso. The smaller foot was immobile and seemed more like a growth than an appendage. The larger left foot appeared to be more functional.

In all other ways, Nick had the sturdy body of a normal boy, as well as a cherubic face any parent would want to kiss and hold. I felt grateful for his lack of awareness, his blissful innocence. I wanted to delay for as long as possible the suffering I feared awaited this child. I placed him back in his hospital crib and walked out into the uncertain future of my family. It seemed like an alternate reality where nothing would ever be normal again.

Wave after wave of overpowering sadness hit me on the drive home. I grieved not for the son who was born but for the son we had expected. I feared that this child would endure a cruel lifetime of suffering. My disbelief and despair flashed to anger. *Why would You do this to us, God? Why?*

Mine was not the response of a superparent or superman. I did not immediately surrender my feelings to God like the Bible's Job, who after losing all his children in a single day calmly said, "The LORD gave and the LORD has taken away."

My response was that of an imperfect, ordinary man, a heartbroken husband and father who wondered if he was somehow responsible for this tragedy, for this incomplete child. Was this a punishment for something I'd done? Many other parents of disabled children have told me they experienced similar doubts, fears, and anger early on.

I worry more about those who don't grieve than about those who do. Professional therapists say we shouldn't stifle our feelings. We should allow them to run their course so that powerful emotions are vented and hopefully pass. This process can be unpredictable, and the patterns vary greatly. Grief is part of the human experience, part of every life, and, I'm sorry to say, part of the journey when expectations for a perfect, healthy child are not met.

The Bible focuses on Job's strength, but I think it likely that he had his moments of crippling weakness as well. All parents want their children to be whole and to have unlimited, hopeful futures. It is quite natural to think that a disabled child will face more difficulties and suffering than others.

We should not be ashamed of expressing our sorrow and allowing our tears to flow. I say this especially for other fathers. Men have this notion that we are tough cookies, that we must shoulder all burdens without complaint or lament. We are socialized not to cry, because emotional displays are seen as a sign of weakness. If we can love, we can hurt. Women and mothers have no monopoly on emotions. Men bond with their children too. They have dreams and expectations for them, just as mothers do. We can be strong and still express our fears and hurt, just as the Bible reveals Jesus often did. There is no shame in that. We all need time to absorb, to adapt, and to adjust.

EXPECTATIONS FOILED

At home I walked into an eerie stillness, an empty house gaily decorated for the anticipated arrival of our firstborn. The baby's room still awaited our son with its cradle and inviting blankets. I recalled feeling concerned when I had assembled the baby bed because I thought the side rails might not be high enough once the baby had the strength to raise himself up. Now all I could visualize was my son lying in bed for the rest of his life, unable to stand, walk, or even crawl. I broke down again, sobbing until exhaustion mercifully plunged me into a troubled sleep.

Morning brought no relief. My body ached from the inside out. I mourned the perfect child we had expected. I grieved for the imperfect child we'd brought into the world. I felt inadequate and incapable of caring for such a child. I felt disconnected from God, who had always sustained me but now seemed to have abandoned me. I did not look forward to returning to the hospital. I dreaded seeing my wife. How could I console Dushka when I felt so lost? How could I face this innocent child, my son, who needed more than I felt capable of providing?

At the hospital I found Dushka awake and awash in tears. I asked her if she'd seen the baby. She could only shake her head.

"Do you want me to bring him to you?"

Another no.

I did my best to console her, staying until she fell asleep, and then I went to the nursery. Again our son was bundled alongside the other babies. He looked quite cute and happy. Looking at his handsome little face, I couldn't help but think, *What kind of life can this child have without limbs? He can't walk, dress himself, feed himself. What will become of him?*

Again anger and remorse welled up within me. *Why, God? Why did You allow this to happen? It would be better for him not to live than to be alive this way. Why don't You take him away and spare him all the pain and suffering?*

I went back to my wife. She had awakened.

She asked me if I'd seen Nick.

"Yes," I replied. "He's a beautiful baby."

She looked away, her face contorting with anguish.

"Do you want me to bring him to you now?"

She shook her head once again and sobbed into her blankets. I had no words to lighten her burden. Our lives had been cut adrift from the reality we'd known and expected.

We were not noble or admirable parents in those few days after Nick's birth. We've told him that, and I think he understands. I certainly hope so.

ALL TOO HUMAN

Even after we'd moved beyond the initial shock, we had to deal with serious doubts about our ability to provide for and care for Nick. One of the factors that worked in our favor during this trying time was the fact that Dushka and I had been married already for five years. We'd waited to start a family while she completed her nursing studies, and then she received additional training as a midwife. I had worked as a clerk and, later, a production planner. We'd had time to travel a little and to save for our first home. Our relationship was well grounded. We were spouses and friends, and we were able to talk most things through to come to an agreement.

Our bond would be tested time and again over the years—as most marriages are. The first major tests came after Nick's birth. Looking back, I believe that Dushka went through postpartum depression, which seemed to compound and extend her initial grief. Every new mother is exhausted after delivering a baby, and most suffer to some degree from mood swings and the "baby blues" brought on by hormonal changes after childbirth. Postpartum depression is a longer-lasting version of this and considered a fairly normal complication. In Dushka's case, it compounded her sorrow and inhibited her ability to come to terms with Nick's lack of limbs.

My loving, caring wife could not cope initially, and she refused to hold Nick or nurse him. Anxiety and fear overcame her. She cried for hours on end, saying, "This can't be real; it has to be a bad dream. I cannot handle this."

Dushka needed time and space to process her emotions. We all handle stress in our own ways. There are common stages of grief—often identified as denial, anger, bargaining, depression, and acceptance—but they can range greatly in intensity and duration. Later I read that when parents learn of a child's illness or disability, they often experience grief in unusual ways. Some go through certain cycles repeatedly or for extended periods. When that happens, they may require therapy.

EMOTIONAL TRAUMA

Recognizing that we are each affected in unique ways can be helpful and reassuring. Spouses need to support each other. Passing judgment isn't helpful. You may think you'd handle the situation or the emotions better, but most people have no grasp of the torment.

During those first few days after Nick's birth, Dushka was overcome in ways that often surprised me because I couldn't fully grasp the depth and breadth of her suffering. On one occasion when I entered her room and found her crying, she whispered, "Don't I deserve flowers like other new mothers?"

Stunned, I responded, "Yes, of course you do! I'm so sorry!"

In all the emotional turmoil, I'd neglected to bring her the traditional gift. I walked out and went down to the hospital flower shop and quickly made amends. Dushka also felt hurt because we hadn't heard from many of our friends and extended family members. I knew they were still processing this unexpected, extraordinary event. Most of them did not know what to say, especially since we hadn't been able to communicate with many of them. Slowly other flowers, gifts, and notes began to trickle in. Most of the comments were very kind and cautious, but my wife and I were often moved to tears as we read them.

When I look back on those times—and when I talk to other parents with disabled children who've gone through similar mourning periods—I can see that Dushka and I did something that is very common. We isolated ourselves during those first days and weeks.

There were several reasons for this. We were hurting and needed time just to be alone to get through the overwhelming emotional turmoil. We didn't want to talk about it at first because that only seemed to make us feel worse. We had no easy words to share, and most of our friends were also uncertain of what to say to us.

We were so caught up in our own feelings that we were blind to the pain of those who loved us. They were hurting too. I had to remind myself that my parents, in-laws, and other family members needed to express their feelings too. In our sorrow, we can lose the ability to empathize with those who are hurting alongside us and for us. We can also forget to be grateful to those who offer kindness and support.

We had a lot to sort out before we could open the door to those who wanted to help us. I encourage other parents who go through these situations to seek help when they are ready for it, because we found that sharing our feelings eased the healing process.

COMING TO TERMS

Dushka is a loving person with strong maternal instincts, but she struggled with accepting Nick's disabilities in those first weeks. I was surprised that after a day or two she still did not want to hold our son, but I came to understand that my wife was not herself.

Seeing that she was distraught, the hospital's social worker delicately laid out our options. She said that if we felt incapable of caring for Nick, we could put him up for adoption.

Initially Dushka was more open to talking about that than I was. We both knew this was a decision we would have to live with for the rest of our days.

I didn't want to give away our son, but I was concerned for my wife. If she didn't feel strong enough to care for Nick even with her nurse's training, how could I demand that she do so? I couldn't tell whether she was so over-wrought because of grief, because she was experiencing postpartum depression, or if it was a combination of both.

Normally the mother is released from the hospital after a couple of days and takes her baby home with her. We did not do that. Our nurses and the hospital's social worker made arrangements for Dushka to stay longer than usual. They also set up a bed for me in her room so we could console each other and talk things through.

The staff felt we needed time together. They talked to us but tried not to rush us to leave or to make hasty decisions. We spent several extra days in the hospital, resting and talking through our emotions, gradually entering into discussions about our next steps.

We had no contingency plan in place, no plan B for a less than perfect baby. After Dushka had rested and gained strength over several days, she told me she was willing to see Nick and hold him. I wasn't so sure she was ready. She still seemed on the edge emotionally. We talked about it, and I realized Dushka also was wracked with guilt. She blamed herself for Nick's disabilities, even though she had done everything by the book during her pregnancy.

At first it was difficult to ease her mind because neither of us had any explanation for Nick's condition. We both had many questions. It would be a while before doctors suggested that Nick's lack of limbs was due to a rare mutation in the genes critical to a child's development in the womb.

CRUEL ENCOUNTERS

Parents of disabled children often remark that they have to develop thick skins. I had my first encounters with this cruel reality shortly after Nick was born. The first was with a person I'd always considered a friend and confidant. I'd often prayed alongside him and shared private thoughts and feelings. I thought he would be sympathetic after Nick was born. I was taken aback when he suggested that my son's disabilities might be God's way of punishing me for my sins.

Honestly, the same thought had occurred to me, though I had no idea what terrible sins I might have committed to merit such a cruel punishment for my innocent child. My friend's words cut deeply and left me reeling for several days. I felt betrayed by his harsh judgment.

I searched my soul to determine if there could be any truth in what he said. We had several frank discussions, and he eventually apologized. I forgave him, and I think in his heart he was trying to be a caring friend all along. Still, he would not be the last person—some well intentioned, others simply clueless—to rock us with insensitive remarks about our son. This was another painful lesson we learned in those early days and one that other parents of special-needs children have experienced: even after the parents have accepted and looked beyond their child's imperfections, it seems most others cannot.

A day or so after Nick's birth, I returned to the pediatric unit nursery to check on our son. I stood at the viewing window and once again found Nick all bundled up, looking like all the other newborns. As I watched, a couple of nurses returned a freshly bathed infant to a nearby cradle, and then they picked up Nick for his examination and bath. They cooed and smiled at him, and he turned on the charm. I know some people say newborns don't really smile, but those people didn't know our little Nick!

For the first time in a couple of days, my heart warmed to our son, and I had a taste of fatherly pride. Then the nurses placed him on an examining table near the back of the room. As they unwrapped him from his swaddling cloth, their expressions changed dramatically. Their eyes went wide, and they put their hands over their mouths at the sight of my son's tiny body.

Once again my heart sank, and I had to walk away from the window. I kept walking all the way out of the hospital, tears streaming. I did not go back to the nursery that day.

COMING TO A DECISION

I understood why they had reacted so strongly to Nick, because Dushka and I had similar responses initially. Up until Nick's birth, neither of us had known or seen an infant without arms or legs, or one with the small, undeveloped feet protruding from his lower torso. It is human nature to be unsettled when first viewing such an unusual body.

While seeing the nurses' reactions was hurtful to a degree, I also felt my paternal protective instincts kicking in. This was my son, and I wanted to shield him from cruelty—intended and otherwise. I also had the growing sense that as little as I knew about raising such a child, no one else would accept and father him like I could.

Dushka and I had not yet made a decision on putting Nick up for adoption, though my heart was telling me all I needed to know. We were coming to terms with our reality. We had some additional time to make up our minds, however, because Nick had a urinary tract infection, and our doctor wanted to keep him a bit longer in the hospital. My wife and I returned to our home, leaving the baby in our doctor's care while we deliberated on the future of our family.

We discussed all our concerns and the options for moving forward. It helped that we came from a similar culture, family background, and faith. I won't say we didn't have disagreements or heated moments. We were under tremendous stress, and we'd both had sleepless nights. Still, we listened to each other.

This had to be a mutual decision. We knew we needed to be on the same page because neither of us could raise Nick on our own. Some of the medical staff had said initially that Nick might not have a normal life span, but Dushka assured me that was not the case, especially if he received proper care and support.

As we weighed our options, Dushka began to emerge from the shadow of sorrow. I knew my wife was back when she began talking less about the challenges of raising Nick and more about finding answers and solutions. She suggested to our medical team that we meet with other parents who had successfully integrated their disabled children into the home. She wanted to know how they coped, what tools they'd found, what adjustments they'd had to make, and how they helped the child deal with everyday life.

Parents of a child born with disabilities are often advised to seek out others who are further along in raising similar children or to join support groups of families in the same situation. We did not have those resources. We could find no other children born like our son. If nothing else, we thought maybe other parents might have found prosthetics, wheelchairs, or other equipment to provide their children some measure of independence.

It would have been so helpful—a miracle, actually—to find an older child with the same challenges as Nick. We might have learned from the parents how to make our child's life easier, what solutions they'd worked out, what resources they'd found to overcome disabilities. Unfortunately this was a miracle that did not come about for us.

MOVING TOWARD ACCEPTANCE

The medical staff told us they could not find anyone born with the same disabilities as Nick. The individuals with most similar disabilities were Australian victims of Thalidomide poisoning. That drug was once used to ease nausea in pregnant women suffering from morning sickness. It was banned once its horrible effects were known.

We were provided contact information for a woman in Melbourne's Beaconsfield Upper area whose daughter had stunted arms and legs. She was then around five years old. We visited this family hoping to gain some insights and maybe even some hope. The girl had enough of each limb to allow her to be fitted with typical prosthetics that would not have been suited for Nick. The only special equipment the child had was a plastic mushroom-shaped stool that she sat upon. By swinging side to side on it, she could make the stool scoot across the floor.

Initially Dushka and I were uncomfortable, and we felt there wasn't much we could learn from this child and her mother. We didn't really benefit so much from talking with them as we did from observing their interactions. It was obvious the mother had limited resources and her daughter had serious disabilities, yet what struck us was their loving relationship and the shocking normalcy of their lives. Neither of them seemed burdened or overwhelmed. They were getting by as best they could without complaint.

I've often thought about that visit and the influence it had on our ultimate decision to raise Nick ourselves. Up to that point, I had a difficult time imagining myself raising a child without limbs as I could foresee only hardship for Nick. The child we visited had severe deformities in her limbs, yet she seemed to be a happy and positive child who did not appear to be overburdened by her disabilities.

The lesson I took away from that visit had quite a lasting influence on me. I learned that rather than being anxious about the future, it was better for us to accept Nick's challenges and deal with them day to day. Jesus taught this principle in His Sermon on the Mount: "But seek first his kingdom and his righteousness, and all these things will be given to you as well. Therefore do not worry about tomorrow, for tomorrow will worry about itself. Each day has enough trouble of its own."

In the same vein, Mark Twain said worrying is like paying a debt you don't owe. We don't want to be so overburdened by what tomorrow might bring that we are robbed of the joys of each day. Yes, we should plan ahead, but there is wisdom also in taking each day as it comes and finding joy in each moment.

I think Dushka and I both saw that the girl and her mother were living in the present, dealing with the challenges as they encountered them, and my wife and I were touched and encouraged by that as we reflected on our visit.

After some additional discussions with our parents and other friends and family, we agreed to take Nick home and do our best for him. In truth, I never thought we would do anything else. He was our child. We went to the hospital the next day and met with the social worker and shared our decision. Once it was done, much of our stress dissipated. We'd been ruminating and fretting over this decision and the potential implications if we went one way or the other. We were relieved to make up our minds and open our hearts to Nick.

One of the Bible verses I read that inspired me during this period featured the story of the angel God sent to Mary. When the angel told the unmarried virgin that she would give birth to a son, she said, "How can this be?" The angel replied, "With God nothing will be impossible."

Dushka and I were at first as incredulous as Mary had been. Then, like her, we decided that our faith could sustain us. With God's help, we could raise this child and help him overcome the many challenges that awaited him. From that point forward, our primary focus was to give Nick everything he needed to become a faith-filled, confident, and self-supporting adult. We never looked back or regretted our decision to raise him, and our love for him grew stronger each day.

TAKEAWAY THOUGHTS

- Be aware that you are grieving, and let it play out.
- Give yourself time to recover emotionally.
- You will need more rest than usual in the early days because of the stress.
- Do not blame yourself or your spouse for your child's disabilities.
- Think about the long term in making early decisions.
- Get all the guidance and advice you can from experts in this field and from other parents.
- Take time to absorb, adjust, and adapt.
- Understand that those close to you are mourning too.
- Your life is changing, but it will be manageable if you take each day as it comes.

Three

A New Normal

Allow Family and Friends to Help You Move Forward

Only a week or so before Nick's birth, a friend had asked me if I thought I could handle raising a disabled child. I don't know what made him think of the question. It certainly surprised me.

My quick response was, "No."

I didn't give his question or my answer any more thought until a few days later when I had to face the reality of raising a child with severe physical disabilities. I was even more terrified than I'd imagined. In my initial despair I even thought of the Bible passages about Jesus praying in the Garden of Gethsemane. He was fearful as He faced dying on the cross for our sins. At one point He prayed, "Father, if it is possible, let this cup pass from Me."

God did not alter the plan for His own Son, and He did not for mine. I had to accept that this was God's plan and hope He would give Dushka and me the strength to see it through. To our everlasting gratitude, He did provide us with the strength, and over time God opened our eyes to what has proven to be a remarkable path for Nick.

FINDING STRENGTH

None of us know what we are fully capable of handling. Most of us underestimate our strength. We often don't factor in the resources available to support us, particularly from our faith, families, friends, and community. Today there are so many more social-service agencies and advocacy organizations for the disabled than there were during Nick's childhood. I wish we'd had more places to turn. I'm glad parents have them now.

We did find that simply taking Nick out of the hospital to our own home made a big difference. We began to regain our equilibrium. Therapists and psychologists who work with families with special-needs children say this usually is achieved by reaching out for support from family, friends, and the larger community. Like many parents, we slowly came to accept our new reality, and then we instinctively worked to create a "new normal." This was an effort to restore balance in our lives. We sought a more positive and proactive environment with lower stress by focusing on acquiring knowledge and finding solutions.

The path to acceptance is not an easy one. It certainly wasn't for my wife and me. As we have explained to Nick over the years, we weren't sad that he was born; we were sorry for the great burden he'd been born with. We also had to deal with a broad assortment of feelings ranging from guilt to inadequacy. Our minds were reeling from all the medical information and decisions we had to make. On top of all that, we were questioning our faith and our God, which meant our primary source of strength was weakened.

It helped that once we returned home, we shifted from merely reacting, which was largely a negative experience, to taking positive actions. Those actions included some routine baby-tending matters like feeding, dressing, and bathing Nick, as well as meeting with medical experts and therapists to educate ourselves on his needs.

The most beneficial step was ending our period of reclusiveness and opening the doors once again to our loved ones, who'd been waiting patiently for the opportunity to reach out and give their support.

Initially Dushka and I had isolated ourselves because we were so over-whelmed. We often talked about feeling as if we were caught in a bad dream and unable to awaken. Sociologists and psychologists refer to feelings of dis-orientation during a crisis as anomie. It is the sense that you've lost your bear-ings and you don't know what to do because so much has changed so quickly. Our experience with Nick proved to be quite typical for parents in our situa-tion, but at the time we didn't have that knowledge to comfort us.

This disorientation was further reinforced by our sudden immersion into an unfamiliar world with its own terminology and language, a world marked by often-grim meetings and intense, sometimes baffling and contradictory conversations with physicians, therapists, and social workers.

We had been staggering through the days and were unable to sleep at nights, haunted by an urgent need to make critical decisions that would have an impact on the rest of our lives. *What are we going to do with this child? How will we do it?*

One of the most common issues faced by the parents of newborns with disabilities is that they don't get to bond as quickly with their children as other parents. Sometimes that is unavoidable because these children often require immediate medical treatment, even surgeries, and then they go to intensive care units.

When Nick was born, doctors and specialists had to assess him. Dushka was also distraught, which limited their time together. Then doctors had to treat Nick's urinary infection, which meant he couldn't go home with us even if we had wanted him to at that point. He remained in the hospital for about four weeks.

Once we had time alone with Nick at home, we were able to bond with him in a natural way that eased our stress. We began to establish our new normal—our life as a family with our unique, ever-surprising baby boy.

REACHING OUT

My advice to other parents in times of crisis is to find ways to bond with your child as early and as often as you can and to fight the urge to go into hiding and dwell on things beyond your control. I understand that it is very difficult to socialize when you are grieving, but those who love you and know you best can handle you at your worst. They may also give you advice that you need but may not want to hear. In our experience, they provided wise counsel and badly needed perspective.

My father was a rock during those early days in Nick's life. While I was a wreck—distraught and panicked—my father was utterly calm and clear eyed. He could not comprehend my emotional turmoil, and he made it clear that he saw no reason to even consider putting Nick up for adoption.

His mind-set was: "Why would you even talk about adoption? This is your child. You are accountable and responsible for raising him. You can handle it. If you can't, we will do it. If you don't have the strength, God will provide it."

My memories of his face during this tormented time are vivid. His jaw was set. His eyes were intense. My father was a disciplined man, especially in times of challenge. He possessed unwavering faith and a powerful moral grip. He expected me to do the right thing, no two ways about it. His belief was that life was not supposed to be easy. Accept that and move on.

He reminded me of Peter's words in the Bible: "Dear friends, don't be surprised at the fiery trials you are going through, as if something strange were happening to you." My father, who had lost his own dad as a child and grew up in poverty, possessed a fortitude forged in hardship beyond my experience and understanding.

His name was Vladimir Vujicic, a strong name for a strong man. He was a warrior, but not the sort of soldier you might imagine. As tough as he was, my dad often reminded us that his name in Serbian means "Peace rules." This might have served as his life's motto. He was drafted by the Yugoslavian army in World War II and served on the front lines as a medic because he followed his Christian faith and declared himself a conscientious objector. He refused to bear arms or kill. His refusal in warfare was met with derision and outrage by many of his superiors and fellow soldiers. They tormented him and tried many times to force him to kill.

My father was frequently transferred to different units in the battlefields, where his job was to retrieve the wounded and treat them. He came under fire, bullets hitting all around him, but he did not fire back. Every time he joined a new unit, there would be guys who resented and challenged him. Dad said one officer told him, "Even if no one else made you fight, I will make you fight. If you don't, I will make you dig your own grave, and I will shoot you on the spot."

"Go ahead and shoot me," my father said. He would not back away from his beliefs.

Another time his superior officers left him alone in camp to guard it. They deliberately left loaded weapons there. When they returned, they hid on the perimeter and ambushed him, firing into their own camp, pretending to be the enemy. They were trying to force him to take up arms to defend himself. He stood his ground even when his life was threatened. They called him a coward, but it took incredible courage for him to remain true to his faith and his beliefs.

GAINING PERSPECTIVE

When we are feeling embattled, in the middle of a crisis or when faced with daunting circumstances, we can easily convince ourselves that our situation is impossibly difficult. Taking a step back to gain perspective can provide substantial relief. My father never lectured me on this. I realized it when he and others of similar backgrounds counseled me on parenting our disabled son. My father's wartime experiences were only one element of a difficult life. He also endured persecution for being a Christian under a Communist dictatorship. At times he and my mother had to attend church services conducted in secret locations. They could have been imprisoned if they'd been caught. They fled to Australia when my father was forty-eight years old and started a new life in a land where they did not speak the language.

My mother was another close example of someone who had endured far greater hardships than I would ever know. Her name was Nada, which in Serbian means "hope." She was always a great sounding board. I could talk to her about anything and everything.

That did not mean she always agreed with me. Like my father—and Dushka's parents too—she believed from day one that we should face up to our responsibilities and take Nick home. She and my father did not understand why we were so tortured. For them it was a given that we would accept our son and raise him.

Dushka's parents, who shared similar backgrounds of hardship, felt the same way. Life was difficult for them in a rural area of war-torn Yugoslavia. The Communist regime imposed severe taxes. Medical and social services were limited. Sanitation was primitive. Two siblings born before Dushka died in infancy. Another child born after her also died.

Her family had to cross the Alps to escape before immigrating to Australia, where things were better but still not easy for them. They expected life to be difficult, and they expected us to shoulder our burdens. My parents reminded me that Jesus told His disciples, "If any of you wants to be my follower, you must turn from your selfish ways, take up your cross, and follow me."

Our parents said that we must be fully committed to Nick and make him the priority in our lives. We respected our parents. They put our challenge with Nick in perspective, and we were humbled. They had dealt with even greater challenges throughout their lives, so why shouldn't we face our own? Dushka and I realized that if our parents could find the strength and courage to overcome all they had dealt with, then we could raise our disabled child.

BONDS OF LOVE

Perspective is an important asset for anyone dealing with hardship and challenges. Over the years, we would be humbled by and impressed with the positive and loving nature of parents whose children had disabilities far greater than our son's. We've learned that most parents with special-needs children find the strength and resources they need.

Many of them feel overwhelmed, exhausted, defeated, fearful, and battered by the unrelenting weight of their responsibilities. Yet their friends and family and all who know them describe them as heroic. Most rise to the occasion. They may have moments of weakness and doubt, but their love for their kids helps them find a way even when there appears to be no way.

In times of personal crisis we tend to think that no one could possibly understand what we are experiencing. Yet nearly every stage of our response to Nick's disabilities was typical for parents dealing with the unexpected challenge of a disabled or special-needs child. They go through grief and disbelief before reaching acceptance. Once that happens, true bonding begins. And when those bonds of love form, the stress diminishes.

Once Dushka and I let go of the child we had expected, and accepted the child God brought to us, we shifted into a more positive outlook. Each day that we were able to hold Nick and see him smile and respond to us served as a steppingstone toward building our family and our lives together.

Our emergence from darkness toward the light actually began as soon as we made the decision to bring Nick home. We immediately felt more in control of our lives. We had come to terms with Nick's disabilities, and once we did that, our mission was to nurture him and make the most of his capabilities.

We had to accept God's will and focus on doing our best, taking each day as it came. When we did that, we found it easier to stop focusing on Nick's "problems" and instead to look for solutions that would give him—and us—the most normal lives we could create. As simple as it sounds, our lives settled down considerably when we stopped worrying about the future, which we could not control, and instead began handling things we could control on a day-to-day basis.

A CHILD ALMOST LIKE ANY OTHER

While Nick is unique physically, he was still in most ways a normal baby. As first-time parents—and as a couple who'd been on their own for five years—we had all the standard adjustments to make, and then a few more. Dushka knew more than I did about caring for infants. I was a rookie at the typical tasks of bottle feeding and diapering. She had to teach me how to take care of Nick in the basic ways, and then we both had to learn about caring for his special needs as a child without limbs.

One early adjustment we made was in the clothing department. Dushka and both of our mothers became custom tailors, staging sewing sessions in which they stitched up the arm and leg holes in all the baby clothes we'd purchased for Nick before he was born. They did have to leave one opening in the legs for his larger foot. By the time they were done, Nick's onesies resembled little straitjackets—something many parents might wish for at times.

Baby Nick seemed to take the confining clothes as a challenge. As he became more active and began crawling and squirming about, our son proved to be an infant Houdini. I don't know how he did it, other than by wriggling and rubbing and squirming, but we had a hard time keeping clothes on him.

Little Nick's eagerness to shed clothing would become a habitual behavior that follows him to this day. It took some time for us to realize that this was a response to the fact that his limbless body had considerably less surface area for venting body heat. Without arms or legs, he easily overheats. Even today, as soon as Nick is out of the public eye, he tends to shed his shirt to stay as cool as possible.

After we'd had a couple more kids, Dushka and I realized that in some ways Nick had been easier to care for than his brother and sister in their first few months. We didn't have to worry about Nick scratching himself with his fingernails, kicking off his blankets, or waking himself up by jerking his arms and legs while dreaming.

Dushka and I had a long-running series of jokes about the fact that we could save a lot of money and time spent redressing him by just letting him go naked. Later we'd note that we saved hundreds in expenditures for baby shoes, socks, and gloves. Our other kids, Aaron and Michelle, were a lot more expensive when it came to clothing, a fact Nick liked to bring up to tease them as they grew older.

Sleep Deprived

There was another common parenting issue we did not have to worry about with baby Nick. Other parents complained that they often woke up in the middle of the night and checked on their silent infants because they worried they weren't sleeping. We never had to check on Nick to see if he was awake because it seemed as though he never slept—and neither did we.

We needed no baby monitor because when Nick was not sleeping, he was crying. This wasn't due to any special issues. He developed the very common, and extremely frustrating, childhood ailment of colic. Marked by crying, restlessness, and general irritability, this isn't considered a serious illness, unless of course you enjoy sleeping or find sleep essential to your sanity.

As many parents know all too well, colicky babies are relentless criers. They can wail on and on for hours. No one really appears to understand what causes colic. It usually strikes between the ages of two weeks and four months. In most cases, it doesn't last more than a couple of weeks. I think Nick had it for several years—okay, maybe it was just a month or so. It's tough to measure time when you don't sleep.

Nick would wake up and begin howling and caterwauling until he collapsed from exhaustion. Dushka and I would pick him up during his crying spells and try to comfort him. Sometimes he'd stop crying for a minute or two, and then, like a relentless car alarm that won't shut off, he'd set off screeching again.

I've never known of a sure cure for colic, but some parents claim that if the child is on baby formula, it can be helpful to change to soy milk. I've known parents who put their babies in car seats placed on top of operating clothes dryers. The vibrations apparently help put them to sleep. Other parents say they've put their colicky kids in the car and driven them around until they go to sleep. Dushka and I did this many times.

As Nick noted in one of his own books, we have a friend who put on noise-dampening headphones and pushed his colicky baby in a stroller around the dining room table until the child stopped crying and fell asleep. That father claimed he made more laps than an Indianapolis 500 driver on some nights.

Dushka and I responded to Nick's colic and his constant crying by parenting in shifts. I took the night shift because I still had a day job. Dushka had the day shift. We were ships passing in the night—two very slow-moving ships with scant wind in our sails.

In my sleep-deprived, slightly addled state of mind during those colicky nights, I found myself wondering if Nick's lack of limbs was somehow contributing to the severity of his colic. I wasn't thinking very clearly, obviously. I also worried that maybe he was crying because he was hungry. He didn't seem to be eating much. I didn't know what to do to calm him. I'd offer him food and hold him, but that raised another issue.

Other parents cautioned that we shouldn't pick up our child every time he cried because he'd come to expect that. It's okay to hold and cuddle your baby, they said, but in most cases you should allow him to cry until he goes to sleep. For a first-time parent with a disabled child, that's not an easy thing to do. My mind tended to create all sorts of worst-case scenarios when I heard my child wailing all the time, even if I knew the colic was to blame.

After a few weeks of torment, Dushka finally took Nick to the pediatrician and explained that no one in our house was sleeping because of our baby's crying jags. The doctor considered this a pretty severe case of colic so he gave us some drops to add to Nick's baby formula. I don't know what medicine or herb it was, but I considered it a miracle drug at the time because the drops calmed him so we all could make it through the night.

For the record, I did not derive any satisfaction or feelings of payback or revenge when—many years later—Nick's own first child developed colic and kept *him* awake for many nights. I'm not that kind of father or grandfather. Maybe I did remind my son of all the sleepless nights he gave us, but I did it with a smile.

I will admit that despite all his crying, there was one thing I enjoyed about Nick's colicky days. For the first time since his birth, I had something normal to complain about in talks with other parents. It was fantastic!

Our friends and family members with children could offer only their sympathies about the challenges posed by Nick's disabilities, but they were more than willing to share their own woes on this subject.

"You're not getting any sleep? Welcome to parenthood!" they'd say.

EMBRACING NORMALCY

We all seek normalcy. We all want to share common experiences. It's part of our need to belong and to be part of something greater than ourselves. That's one of the reasons having a disabled child threw us off so much initially. We lost our bearings because we had expectations of a normal child and a normal parenting experience. Having a child with no limbs placed us outside the realm of our shared experiences.

Most of us are wary or fearful of challenging experiences unless we're seeking them. When we are forced into situations that are outside our comfort zone, we tend to feel stressed and beleaguered. In those situations, our instinct is to try to regain a sense of normalcy.

For parents with disabled newborns, this often means redefining what is normal for their family by establishing new comfort zones. Dushka and I expressed this when we said things like "We just want to get our lives back" or "We want to be a normal family again."

We often wondered at first if we would ever return to a comfortable existence. Yet the more time we spent with our son, the more we embraced our new life. It helped us tremendously to surround ourselves with other members of our family who were ready by then to welcome Nick into our rather large fold.

Dushka had nine kids in her family. I grew up with five siblings. Then there were cousins and other extended family members, along with many members of our church who were like family to us. We had quite a substantial community of supporters, but they'd been careful and thoughtful, giving us time to adjust. Although they were eager to offer assistance, they held back until we were ready to ask for it.

This may sound a little strange, but our lives had changed so dramatically that we were a bit surprised to discover that our circle of family and friends was still intact. The environment hadn't changed as much as we had feared. They were still there for us. They were eager to encourage us. Dushka and I felt like we were stepping into a warm and inviting home after weeks of wandering lost in a cold and hostile landscape.

I had some initial reticence about socializing again because I thought no one would be able to understand what we'd been through. I worried that we wouldn't know what to say to each other or that Nick's unusual body would make them unwilling to hold him or interact with him. I was heartened, then, to find that most relatives and friends were empathetic and quite eager to welcome Nick. To see the important people in our lives coddle and hug him was comforting and encouraging.

Once Nick was over the colic, his true demeanor emerged, and everyone was charmed by his sweet-natured, smiling, and determined attitude. He was actually quite adorable. Even back then, I observed our infant son win over complete strangers with his abundant charms. For those who spent even a brief time with him, Nick's lack of limbs didn't define him as much as his exuberant and engaging personality did. He loved to be held and coddled and was quite verbal and expressive.

Nick was born into a large brood of about thirty cousins, most of them rowdy males, and they proved to be a blessing in many ways as they grew up together. From infancy through childhood and to this day, Nick's boisterous cousins have accepted him, loved him, relentlessly teased him, tossed him about (to my frequent terror), and generally treated him as one of the gang.

Each of our family members was positive and encouraging and relieved that we were home with our son. All of them made it clear they were willing to step up and give support whenever and however we needed it.

Returning to the embrace of our relatives and friends helped us heal and come together as a family. Dushka and I could have handled basic things like feeding, bathing, and clothing our son after taking him home. But having others in our lives who loved our son provided the support we needed to heal emotionally.

ON THE OTHER SIDE OF GRIEF

As family and friends bonded with Nick, our own love and acceptance of him deepened. Late at night or in the early mornings when I had time to reflect, I wished we could have reached this stage of acceptance sooner and without so much pain. It would have been helpful to understand that we would eventually find strength so that we could settle into a new normal, a place beyond sorrow that was less stressful and more like the life we had expected.

Pregnancy is a vulnerable time for women emotionally, and it's important to stay positive and hopeful. I suppose social workers, therapists, and physicians don't want to alarm or burden expectant parents with stressful thoughts, and that's understandable. There is probably not ever a good time to counsel expectant parents on the possibilities of delivering a disabled child. Still, I did find myself wishing that we had been prepared in some way or that we'd had someone who could pull back the black curtain and show us that more hopeful, more normal days awaited us on the other side.

I don't want to give the impression that as soon as we took Nick home we were suddenly free of anxiety about his future. We still had sleepless nights even after his colic was gone. Yet during this period, we were able to breathe a little easier and feel more like typical parents.

After we took Nick home and worked through his bout with colic, I felt the stirrings of a greater confidence. Like many parents in that situation, I learned to take the challenges as they came and to rely on God's strength whenever I felt weak. We just don't know our full capacity for overcoming and persevering until we are fully challenged and everything is on the line. Then, and only then, do we discover what lies within us.

When Dushka and I accepted the challenge of raising Nick, we did it with humility and prayers, which was the wisest thing we could do because we definitely felt in over our heads. We are all vulnerable, and so we should all remain humble and faithful. This was the lesson also in the Bible story of the apostle Peter. He considered himself the most loyal disciple of Jesus. When Jesus was under threat of arrest and persecution, Peter boasted that when others denied and abandoned Jesus, he would stand and fight to the death for Him.

Jesus told Peter that before the night was over, Peter would deny Him three times. Peter insisted that this would not happen, but it did, just as Jesus predicted. I feel that both Dushka and I came apart when the reality of life hit us with the birth of a limbless child. We had our great expectations all set. We were ready for that "perfect" newborn child. We felt confident, like Peter, that we were strong and unwavering in our faith. And then when Nick arrived, we were devastated and all our joy was gone because he had no limbs. Our faith was shaken. Our lives were thrown into turmoil.

I'm thankful I'd admitted to my friend days before that I felt unequal to the task of raising a disabled child. Still, in many ways I certainly felt like Peter because I was so much weaker than I'd expected. I was a church elder who had preached and taught others to trust God and His promises. There's definitely an expectation that church leaders should not only preach but also live and demonstrate these virtues and qualities. Yet people forget that church leaders are human and that they experience the same difficulties as everyone else. I came to see that part of God's plan was to keep me aware of how much I need Him in my life.

God promises His support in the Bible when He says He will never leave us or forsake us. This is the lesson I had to learn: rely on God and His power. Dushka and I leaned on each other, on our faith, and on our family, as well as our entire community of supportive friends. We still had fears for Nick's future, but we chose to focus on the daily process of caring and providing for him.

There was one other powerful source of strength who surprised us nearly every day in our journey. Many parents of special-needs children discover, as we did, that it is our children themselves who become our greatest inspirations. In the next chapter, I reveal how our son became our hero.

TAKEAWAY THOUGHTS

- Resist the urge to isolate yourself.
- Accept the support of family and friends.
- As quickly as possible move from a reactive position to being proactive.
- Establish new daily routines.
- Return to doing "normal things," including work, socializing, and recreation.
- Find support groups, online forums, and other sources of information.

Four

Blessed Are
His Children

Let Your Child
Be Your Guide

Nick was only eighteen months old when we traveled to the United States to attend a summer church camp in Virginia. One hot and sticky night near the end of the week, Dushka and I were taking Nick back to our dorm room from dinner when a guy I'd never met walked up to us.

"When are you going to take off your mask?" he said.

"What do you mean?" I replied.

He pointed a finger at Nick, who was wearing just a diaper and no shirt because of the heat.

"Why do you act like everything is fine?"

Apparently he was mortified that our son wasn't covered up. He seemed to think we should conceal Nick's body as if we were ashamed of him.

"I don't know what mask you're referring to," I said. "We are the way we are, just as you see us."

He walked away shaking his head. I don't think this person at the church camp meant to be cruel or offensive when he asked me that question. He probably hadn't been around many people with physical disabilities, because once you spend time with them, you gain a different perspective. They teach you to see beyond their challenges and into their hearts.

He may have been blunt or even rude in confronting us, but I actually felt some gratitude toward the stranger later. He reminded me of how far I had come in my acceptance of Nick's disabilities since his birth. When I thought about our journey, I realized the biggest influence was Nick himself. He taught us how to accept and love him, which always reminds me of Jesus's words in Matthew 18:2–6:

> He called a little child to him, and placed the child among them. And he said: "Truly I tell you, unless you change and become like little children, you will never enter the kingdom of heaven. Therefore, whoever takes the lowly position of this child is the greatest in the kingdom of heaven. And whoever welcomes one such child in my name welcomes me."

Nick taught us that he was not a "lowly" or disabled child. Instead, he was a child with disabilities that could be overcome with patience, creativity, and the healing power of love. We learned acceptance from Nick, who proved to be our greatest source of inspiration and enlightenment.

When he was born, we saw only his disabilities at first. He taught us that his lack of arms and legs would never define him or even slow him down all that much. Over the years, I've heard other parents of special-needs kids talk about recognizing their children as individuals who are not defined by their disabilities. We see quickly that they may have unique challenges, but their disabilities are just a small part of who they are.

THE CHILD AS TEACHER

Jesus was twelve years old when He strayed off from Mary and Joseph and other relatives as they returned home to Nazareth from the festival of Passover in Jerusalem. Three days passed before they found Him back in the temple "sitting among the teachers, listening to them and asking them questions," according to the Bible.

You do have to wonder how Joseph and Mary could lose their child for three days. Nowadays they might have been jailed and tormented on social media for letting their child run wild. The Bible doesn't mention any criticism. We're told that everyone who heard the young Jesus speak in the temple was amazed at His depth of understanding and knowledge. Joseph and Mary were undoubtedly surprised to see that their Son already had a strong sense of His purpose on earth.

From an even earlier age, our son had a similar impact on Dushka and me, and everyone who encountered him. Today people often tell Nick that within minutes of meeting him, they are so engaged by his personality that they lose any awareness of his disability. Dushka and I understand this completely. Beginning in infancy, Nick taught us to see beyond his physical abnormalities to the dynamic and determined person who simply refused to accept a life limited in any way by his lack of limbs.

The point can be made that our experience with Nick is different from those of parents with more severely disabled children, such as those with severe mental impairments or limited ability to communicate. Yet Dushka and I have met many parents of children with Down syndrome, autism, and other more debilitating disabilities, and those men and women report similar experiences.

Fathers tend to think they will mold their children, especially their sons, into the people they want them to be. The truth is that, in most cases, our children teach us who they are and how to love them unconditionally. The man who stopped me in the church camp that evening did not understand that Nick was already guiding us not only to love him but also to be proud of him and to be grateful that he is our son.

This was a great gift to us. The lesson is one we have shared with many other parents of disabled kids. One father I've helped mentor in recent years has a son who, like Nick, is without limbs. This father once told me that it bothered him when people stared at his son or made comments about his lack of limbs. He felt guilty about his response.

"Should I keep him covered when I take him out in public?" he asked.

I understood that he was trying to protect his son from being hurt, but, as I told him, Dushka and I concluded that trying to hide Nick's disabilities might cause him more harm than good. We didn't want Nick to think we were embarrassed or ashamed of him. We knew that one day he would likely have to deal with people who rejected him, bullied him, or mocked him because of his disabilities. Our goal was to build upon his natural inclination to rise above his lack of limbs and to live as normally as he could. Nick was not easily daunted by his disabilities. He inspired us to deal as courageously with them as he did.

Sadly not every parent reaches acceptance. Some run away from their disabled child, their marriage, and their responsibilities. The impact on the children and on the entire family can be devastating when one or both parents turn inward or flee. I've heard of fathers who become workaholics so they don't have to deal with a disabled child at home. Others turn to drugs or alcohol to self-medicate because they can't escape the "Why me?" questions, their grief, their guilt, or their feelings of inadequacy.

This is tragic. I don't judge them, but I fear they will never learn how much their children can teach them about themselves, about life, courage, and unconditional love. The trap many mothers and fathers fall into is that they think they have to become superparents who have all the answers, energy, and hopefulness their children will ever need. Most of us just aren't that wonderful, but we don't have to be. We only have to do our best, have faith, and lean on our loved ones and whatever other support we can find. We allow our children to lead us to understanding.

FOLLOWING NICK'S LEAD

Jesus taught a very valuable lesson about cherishing and taking care of today only. In the Bible, He asked, "Can any one of you by worrying add a single hour to your life? . . . Therefore do not worry about tomorrow, for tomorrow will worry about itself."

This was the first lesson we had to learn. We expected at first that raising a disabled child might be a daily grind, a struggle, and an exhausting journey. It was not any of those things, mostly because of Nick himself. Thanks to his unstoppable spirit, it's been a revelation. Our experiences with him have given us a much deeper awareness of the value of every human being, as well as a richer appreciation for life's blessings and the staggering power of God's presence in our lives.

My wife and I were not alone in our fight to create the best possible life for our child. Nick was eager to do all he could as well. Medical experts, psychologists, and therapists gave us their advice on what Nick needed, but in truth, he was our best source of information and inspiration. At nearly every stage of his development, Nick proved to be far more self-reliant than we had ever anticipated. We learned not to make assumptions about what he could and could not do, and we joined him in rejecting any labels others placed upon him.

Disabled children are every bit as individualized as normal children. They have much to learn from us, but they can also teach us a great deal— about their needs, their potential, their ability to overcome challenges, and the strength of their spirits. It is not unrealistic to expect that a disabled child may have severe limitations, but it is also true that many of them rise above and beyond expectations.

As we settled into life with Nick, his mother and I gradually came to the realization that there existed two sharply different outlooks in our family.

Dushka and I tended to hover over our son, fretting about him, worrying that he might be sick or hungry, that he might injure himself or be injured by someone else.

Baby Nick, on the other hand, was blissfully unaware of his stressed-out helicopter parents. He was a smiling, happy, and quite energetic little guy, who seemed not the least bit troubled by his lack of limbs.

Slowly it dawned on us that since Nick was born without limbs, he didn't miss having them. Nick was like most infants at that stage of development. None of them move around much. They all have to be fed and bathed. We took care of all that for him, just as any other parents would for a newborn. This period gave us time to feel like normal parents, and it also allowed us more opportunities to learn Nick's personality and to bond further with him.

Dushka knew the typical stages of development for infants, including the first three to nine months when most babies become strong enough to lift their heads while lying on their stomachs, then begin to roll over, sit up, and crawl. Children tend to do this at their own pace, of course, but most kids master these maneuvers within the first year.

We didn't know what to expect with Nick. He could lift his head while lying on his back at three months or so—he seemed to have quite the strong neck—but we weren't sure how he'd do in the next stages of development because he lacked limbs that usually provide leverage for rolling over and crawling.

This was a big concern for us. Dushka knew that crawling is an important milestone with far more significance than mere locomotion. It serves to stimulate brain development and also prepares the brain for learning. While crawling, the child has to make decisions on direction. Normally this gives physicians an early measure of the infant's hand-eye coordination, an important factor in everything from reading and writing to catching and kicking. Crawling is important also for the development of vision, as the infant's gaze moves from looking ahead to looking back down at his hands and the path in front of him.

FOOT-SHOULDER COORDINATION

We saw these early milestones as tests of our son's ability to compensate for his lack of limbs. We wondered if he would have the mental capacity, adaptability, strength, and determination to develop his own methods for mobility. I still harbored fears that Nick might have to spend his life in bed. We had been told to expect that he might not begin to roll around, sit up, or crawl within the typical four- to eight-month time frame. Yet he was not a lethargic baby; in fact, he was very active, always moving his torso and squirming about. After his first few months, we would go to his crib and find that he had somehow repositioned himself. This gave us our first indications that Nick would not be content just lying in his bed. From that point on, every indication of mobility was a cause for excitement.

We were learning that even when doctors said there was no way, our son would come up with "Nick's way." When we picked him up and held him upright, we could feel that Nick was actually quite a strong little guy. He'd wiggle about and then show us that he could hold himself upright in a sitting position. He was quite pleased with himself, and we clapped enthusiastically to show him we were pleased as well.

Nick's progression was slower than children with limbs, but once he got rolling, there was no stopping him. He was nearly a year old before I first saw him shift from his back to his side in his crib. He had been turning his head and lifting it up from a face-down position for a while. Then one day, I saw him rocking back and forth, using his larger foot for leverage against the mattress. After a few unsuccessful trials, he succeeded in flipping himself onto his side. This was exciting, encouraging, and comforting all at the same time.

NICK'S WAY

We were thrilled to see that he was not content to lie flat, and even more grateful that our boy was active and ingenious at finding his own solutions. He amused us early on by using his larger foot to spin himself around and around on the tile floor. It was our first hint that this foot would serve him in many ways. He also used it to play with toys we'd put in his crib. Some of them made sounds or played music when rolled around, and Nick quickly picked up on this. He learned to use the foot to compensate for his lack of arms and hands and quickly became adept at manipulating it. He'd play with toys by moving them about with his feet, delighting in the sounds and movement his efforts produced. There were a couple of toys with holes of various shapes, and he'd stick his foot into the openings to pick them up, shake them, and toss them around.

He seemed to delight in the bright colors and musical sounds. Dushka and I got the sense that Nick was just as eager to show us what he could do as we were to explore his capabilities. His increasing activity, his alertness, and his growing vocabulary of baby babble heartened us. This all seemed to indicate that he was not impaired mentally, and in fact, he appeared to be quite a sharp little guy.

I wish the doctors who had given us dark forecasts for Nick's development could have observed him as a baby, mastering ways to move about without benefit of arms or legs. Dushka and I were inspired, touched, and thrilled as we watched our baby boy lie flat on the floor, then brace himself by placing his forehead on the carpet, and arch his back until he could scoot his lower body forward, slowly raising his body. Later he figured out a way to accomplish this by bracing his forehead against the couch or a wall. We never would have come up with that method; instead, he figured things out himself.

Neither of us realized it at first, but our attitude toward our son was evolving. We were becoming quite proud of his accomplishments. You could say we were his most enthusiastic cheerleaders. We still saw ourselves as his protectors and guides, but we also were discovering that our son had a lot to teach us. This was all part of a shifting focus from seeing our son's disabilities and limitations—the things he could not do—to marveling at his abilities. Most parents experience this in some way. I was reminded of this just recently when I saw the photographs taken by a young Utah father of his toddler with Down syndrome. Alan Lawrence has created a blog (www.thatdadblog.com) to share his journey with his fifth child, Wil.

This dad was candid in admitting that when Wil was diagnosed with Down's, he responded with fear and disappointment. Lawrence said all he could think about was that Wil would strain the family's resources and be a burden. He was so ashamed at first that he refused to share baby photos with family and friends.

But then little Wil taught his father that Down syndrome did not define him. By the time he was a toddler, Wil's loving and gleeful spirit had won over his entire family. Instead of feeling burdened or ashamed, the Lawrences felt uplifted and proud of Wil.

The exuberant toddler entertained his parents and brothers and sisters with his antic movements while lying on the floor or crawling about. He would wave his arms and legs as if attempting to fly like a superhero. To capture Wil's soaring spirit, his father began creating photographic images that were altered to make it appear that Wil was soaring in the air above family members as they biked, hiked, explored nature, and went about their daily lives.

At first Lawrence, an art director, just published the heartwarming photos on his blog, but they drew such a strong positive response that they were soon picked up and published by media outlets all over the world. The family photos of Wil went viral, inspiring Lawrence to create more images and a calendar designed to increase understanding of Down syndrome and compassion for children like Wil. "I want other parents just starting out this journey . . . to have a more positive outlook on it than I did," Lawrence said in one published interview.

I'm sure Alan Lawrence will learn, as I have, that our special children continue to surprise us with their capabilities throughout their lifetimes. This has been the experience also of D. L. Hughley, who is widely known as a comedian and television sitcom star, and the father of son Kyle, who was born with Asperger's syndrome. Now in his late twenties, Kyle continues to surprise and inspire his father, who told of one learning experience in an interview on the television show *Oprah: Where Are They Now?*

Hughley said Kyle managed to get a college degree, but he remained very cautious and regimented. He did not like to try new things, so Hughley was surprised one day when his son volunteered to put gas in the car after they stopped at a filling station.

It was unusual for his son to volunteer to do something he'd never attempted on his own, so when Kyle got out of the car and went to the pump, Hughley was "a nervous wreck." When Kyle returned to the car and happily gave his father the credit-card receipt and the car keys, Hughley broke down sobbing. He told Oprah on her show that it was because Kyle did something he'd always been afraid to do. "I just didn't believe he could do it. He did it. And I held him and I said, 'You're going to be all right.'"

EXCEEDING EXPECTATIONS

Dushka and I can relate to those experiences, as can most other parents with special-needs kids. We learned early on with Nick that it was wise not to bet against him or to place any sorts of limits on him. Time and again, he not only proved us wrong; our son flat out amazed us.

In the spring of 2015, Nick posted a video on his Facebook page that serves as a perfect illustration of this point in several ways. First of all, when Nick was born without limbs, we never dreamed he would be able to move about on his own. Second, we thought it was highly unlikely he would ever marry. Third, we thought he would never have children.

This joyful video demonstrates that we were dead wrong on all accounts. It's just a brief clip (www.youtube.com/watch?v=qU5TrnR1meY), but it begins with Nick madly scampering into view with his giggling son Kiyoshi bounding after him, catching him, hugging him, giving a quick kiss, and then scampering off to continue their game of hide-and-seek. It's a simple moment, but it's especially poignant and powerful when you consider that we had so little hope for our son when he was first born.

The child whose birth made us despair has proven to be such an incredible blessing. This particular video is one of hundreds of inspiring videos Nick has done. They all serve as testimonials to how foolish it is to place limits on our disabled and special-needs children. By the way, just a few hours after that particular video was posted, admirers around the world had viewed it more than 1.5 million times.

Running Without Limbs

When Nick was an infant, we were delighted that he could roll over, sit up, and stand just a few months behind what is considered normal. Dushka and I had doubted that our son without legs would be able to achieve mobility on his own. So imagine our surprise when Nick began moving about the house upright and walking. We couldn't even figure out how he was doing it at first. After observing him, we saw that he used his larger foot to raise himself up and then rotated his hips to move forward. If he did this slowly, there was a barely perceptible hop to his motion. When he went faster, it was like a gallop.

I am always touched when Nick talks about his recurring dreams of running at full speed through a field and about what a joy it would be to do that one day. The truth is that he can dart about quickly on his own for short distances. His brother and sister and cousins will attest that as a youngster he was quite the competitor in their rough-and-tumble living room soccer matches. In that confined area, Nick was pretty much equal to them all.

Dushka and I were grateful for his mobility and his determination but also more than a little concerned that Nick would injure himself or be injured by his playmates. He was so aggressive and uninhibited in his play that other children forgot about Nick's vulnerability. If he fell, he didn't have arms to catch himself or to protect his head from hitting the floor or furniture. I was a bit of a wet blanket at times, always cautioning Nick and the other kids not to play so rough and to be careful. Of course, none of them paid much heed to old worrywart me. As Nick would say, "Dad, it's not like I'm going to break an arm or a leg!" He did manage to get through childhood without any serious injuries, even though he took some nasty falls.

As an adult, Nick often tells stories of his daredevil exploits like surfing, skydiving, and snowboarding. He's also been known to have his friends and caregivers deposit him in overhead compartments on airplanes to frighten other passengers or to place him on baggage carousels as a prank. Rest assured, this sort of behavior didn't begin in adulthood—he was fearless and uninhibited from the start.

One of his favorite childhood pastimes was racing up and down the neighborhood streets while lying on a skateboard, often towed behind the bicycles of his brother and other playmates. I'm glad I didn't know until years later that they would sometimes mount him on their handlebars and wheel him around all day.

A Most Difficult Lesson

For most of Nick's childhood, he was an upbeat, positive, and irrepressible youngster. He was a source of joy for everyone around him. Yet if you are familiar with Nick's journey, you are likely aware that in childhood and even in adulthood he has had occasional bouts of despair and depression. This is often an area of concern for people with disabilities, but in all candor Dushka and I were caught off guard when Nick first began having dark thoughts as a child.

Despite his fun-loving demeanor, Nick has a very serious and contemplative side. Even as a child he would engage us in conversations with thoughtful questions that were surprising in their maturity and depth. He was probably around eight or nine when he first asked us why he was born without limbs, what caused them not to grow, why God had made him that way, and how we felt when we first learned he had no limbs.

Dushka and I knew these questions would come one day, and we had decided to be truthful with him because we feel that honesty and transparent relationships are important for integrity and true love. Children are very sensitive and quickly pick up on family dynamics and stories even when we think they're too young yet to understand. We knew Nick might find out one day about our emotional upheaval at his birth, and we wanted to be the ones to tell him the full story. We strived to protect him and assure him that he was loved and valued.

The goal was to gently share the fact that although at first we were aggrieved and fearful because of his disabilities, we quickly came to love him. Dushka did tell him also that we briefly considered putting him up for adoption, but only because we weren't certain we had the ability to cope or the resources and knowledge necessary to raise a child without limbs.

At first Nick was hurt when told of our initial concerns after he was born, but we talked through it, and we felt that even if he didn't fully understand right away, he would come to terms with it as he grew older. We always emphasized how much we loved him and how proud we were of him. Still, it was just a short time after that heart-to-heart talk that Nick gave us cause for concern about his private thoughts and his emotional state.

His younger brother, Aaron, came to me one night in his pajamas just after we'd put the boys to bed. He seemed very upset. He said Nick had just told him something scary. "Dad, you better talk to Nick. He just told me that he'd probably kill himself by the time he is twenty-one," Aaron said.

Nick often would descend into darker moods and serious thoughts at night when he was tired, but I'd never heard him say anything as alarming as this. Mortified, I hurried back to their room, sat beside Nick in his bed, stroked his thick mop of blond hair, and asked him what was on his mind.

He then began asking the sort of what-if questions that parents often dread.

"What if something happened to you or Mum? Who would look after me?"

"What if I could never get a job? How would I support myself after you were gone?"

"Do you think I'll ever get married and have a family of my own?"

These are difficult and emotional questions for any parent. I gently talked with Nick about his fears and doubts, wishing I had a magic wand to dispel his very legitimate concerns. It seemed I was making some headway soothing him, until my son revealed to me that he had harbored suicidal thoughts and impulses to act upon them.

"I have thought it would be better to just kill myself so you and Mum and Aaron and Michelle could have normal lives. The other day I was up on the kitchen counter, and I thought about throwing myself off, but I wasn't sure if it was high enough to actually kill me," he said tearfully. "I just can't stand the thought that I'll always be a burden on you and Mum or on Aaron and Michelle."

Oh my! I was stunned but tried to control my own emotions while calming him. I did my best to reassure him. I cuddled and held him close. I told him that even though we would be gone at some point, there would always be family, extended family, and friends to help and support him if he needed them.

"There are many people who love you, Nick. And most of all there is God who loves you more than us all. He will provide all you need if you hold Him in your heart," I said.

I reassured him that we loved him and would miss him. That night, I did all I could to let him know that our initial concerns and fears at his birth quickly had given way to a deep love for him and that we believed he had a bright future. After our talk, Nick seemed reassured. I made him promise to come to me anytime he had concerns.

Still, I didn't sleep well that night or for many nights. Dushka and I discussed ways we could build a stronger emotional foundation for our son to prevent any further suicidal thoughts. We kept a close eye on him in the months that followed, making sure to give him hugs and reassure him every night.

FRIGHTENING REVELATION

When Nick revealed his suicidal urges to us that night, we had no idea he had actually made a suicide attempt. He did not tell us that until a dozen years later, during the writing of his first book, *Life Without Limits.* He had decided to reveal the suicide attempt in the book because he wanted it to serve as a cautionary tale to other young people. Suicide had become a major issue, especially for teens, and Nick felt it was his responsibility to speak out. His primary message was that life is a gift and that there is always reason to hope for a better tomorrow. His own life serves as a wonderful example that God's plan for us is often beyond our wildest dreams.

While writing this in his book, Nick realized he needed to prepare us, so he told us the story for the first time. We were stunned when he gave us the details. On the afternoon prior to telling us of his suicidal urges, he had actually made several attempts to drown himself in the bathtub.

How could we have missed this? Where were we when he needed us?

Nick filled us in on the frightening details. He'd begun experiencing nagging feelings of hopelessness and despair a few years earlier. For years he had prayed every night, asking God to give him arms and legs. He could not fathom how a loving God could deprive him of limbs, and that led him to question both his faith and his worthiness.

It was around this time that Nick first experienced bullying and cruel remarks at school. While he was adept at fitting in and doing many things that other kids did, Nick could not escape the thought that he'd never be able to compete in sports, hold hands with a girlfriend, or hold his children in his arms.

He had growing fears about his future, including his ability to support himself as an adult and whether he'd ever marry and have a family. He'd reached the age when other boys were finding girlfriends, and Nick feared no girl would like him because of his lack of limbs. Our son said he feared he would be a burden to us for his entire life.

Wave after wave of dark thoughts tormented him, and he couldn't shut them out. He'd catch himself thinking things like, *If I just jumped off this countertop, I would probably die in the fall and could end it all now.* It's very scary for me to consider that our son was thinking that way and we didn't know it.

A LIFE AT RISK

Nick later told us that he tried to fight off the self-destructive urges, but they were unrelenting. Dogged by thoughts that he should just end his life rather than continue on, he decided to drown himself in the bathtub. He asked me to fill it with water, pretending he just wanted to bathe and chill out a bit, as he'd done so often. When I left the room, he immersed himself and made several attempts to stay underwater.

Gratefully, Nick couldn't go through with it. Visions of Dushka, Aaron, Michelle, and me grieving kept filling his mind. He knew that his suicide would haunt us for the rest of our lives, and in the end Nick decided he could not do that to his loved ones.

You can imagine how difficult it is for me to even write about this. To think that we nearly lost Nick is just terrifying. We can't imagine life without him, and it has taken us a long time to get over the guilt we feel that he even considered suicide as a child. In our talks with him about this near tragedy, however, we realized that Nick did not follow through with his suicide attempt because we had done something right: he knew we loved him and that losing him would torment us for the rest of our lives.

Nick told us that his love and concern for us was more powerful than his despair. In retrospect, I think Nick told Aaron about his suicidal thoughts because he knew in his heart that his brother would come to us. I believe Nick wanted us to know. He wanted our help and intervention.

For that, we are all grateful, of course, yet the depth of Nick's despair at such a young age haunts us still. We will never again assume that we fully comprehend the burden he carries, even as he inspires millions around the world. He has had periods of depression since that episode, even as a young adult. Most of them occurred when he was exhausted from his world travels, lonely and hurt because of failed relationships, or overwhelmed by business and financial pressures. My son has a tendency to take on many burdens because he has so much faith in himself and in God. We are always encouraging him to take more time off with his family, which is where he finds the most joy and peace.

You may think you know your child and your child's mind, but as we learned in our son's case, a child with severe disabilities can have a very complex and secretive emotional life. Our experience with Nick's suicidal thoughts taught us some important lessons:

- It is important to always keep open the lines of conversation with children and to actively engage with them as often as possible to get a read on their emotional lives. It's often said that you should listen even to the unimportant things they have to say so that they'll come to you with the truly important things later.

- No matter how well we may think we know our children, there are secrets and hidden corners in their minds that we may have difficulty detecting and understanding. Parents need to be informed about warning signs, alert to dark thoughts, and prepared to seek professional guidance.

- We must never take lightly expressions of fear or despair about the future. When your child speaks of these things, even in jest, it is a cry for attention and a warning sign to address his or her emotional life.

Experts say that for most people with disabilities, suicidal thoughts spring not so much from any physical challenges but more from bullying, social ostracism, and their concerns about being a burden to their loved ones. The

American Association of Suicidology reports that teenagers with dyslexia are more likely than normal readers to think about and attempt suicide. Penn State researchers found that the rate of suicidal thoughts and attempts among autistic children is twenty-eight times greater than for typical children.

Nick's attempted suicide taught me that no matter how close you may feel to your children—and no matter how well you think you are communicating with them—there is still room for darkness to creep into their hearts and minds. Dushka and I had felt we were doing everything to the best of our abilities in protecting Nick and monitoring his emotions and behavior, but kids can put up a facade of happiness and well-being even when they are going through dark periods.

PROTECTING OUR CHILDREN

Feelings of discouragement or despair can escalate quickly, change our perspectives, and convince us that our lives lack value or meaning if we don't take measures to counter those thoughts. Children are just as vulnerable as adults and probably more so because they may not know where to turn. Parents should keep that in mind and be alert for any signs of mood shifts, changes in eating patterns, withdrawal from friends and family, and other uncharacteristic behaviors.

Today Nick is considered one of the most prominent voices speaking out against suicide to young people around the world. Educators and government leaders in the United States, Europe, and Asia invite him to address young audiences to give them hope and encouragement. Thousands of people have told him that his speeches and videos have helped them overcome self-destructive thoughts and urges.

His story is a cautionary tale for us all, especially the parents of special-needs boys and girls, men and women. Despair and depression are insidious threats. We never know when they will twist the thinking of those we love, but we can always make sure our children know they are loved and appreciated.

A pastor once told a story about a woman in his congregation who complained to him that her husband did not love her. Every time they met, she complained about his lack of attention. Finally the pastor called the husband in for counseling.

"Your wife has been sharing concerns with me that you don't seem to love her or care for her anymore," the pastor said.

The husband replied, "Pastor, on the day we were married, I told her I loved her. When that changes, I will let her know."

I'm afraid it doesn't work that way with spouses or with our children! Just because you work hard or do things for them, you cannot assume that those you care about know the depth of your feelings or that they don't need to be reminded. They need our hugs and kisses. They need us to be interested in their lives and to spend time with them.

Giving time to your kids is the greatest gift you can provide. Talk to your children and let them know they can confide in you or ask you whatever is on their minds. Stay close, keep your ears and eyes open, and listen intently with the desire to understand their perspective. By allowing our children to show us who they are and what they need from us, we all enjoy richer and more rewarding relationships.

TAKEAWAY THOUGHTS

- Understand that your child is a complex individual not defined by disabilities or labels.
- Let your child teach you who she is, how she can be reached, and the meaning of unconditional love.

- Focus on what your child can do rather than what he cannot do. Encourage and support your child by allowing him to set his own pace.
- Keep the lines of communication open and always assure your child that she is loved and valued. Do not assume she is okay even if she says she is.
- Monitor your child's moods closely and stay in regular contact with his teachers, especially in the preteen and teen years.

Five

The Medical Maze

Become Chief Advocate for Your Child's Medical Care

My nephew, Nate Polijak, is a registered nurse in Australia. During training for that job, he got in a bit of hot water because of his cousin Nick. Nate's instructor was teaching the class how to take a patient's blood pressure. When the instructor asked if the students had any questions, Nate thought of Nick and asked, "What if the patient has no arms?"

"Then you would use a vein in the thigh," the instructor said.

"But what if the patient has no legs?" Nate said.

"Okay, wise guy, why don't you get out of here!" demanded the instructor.

He kicked Nate out of class. Nate did have a reputation as a joker, and he had to talk fast to convince his teacher that he was asking these questions out of concern for his cousin Nick, who had neither arms nor legs.

Parents often joke that they wish their babies arrived with specific operating instructions. In our case, this was no joke, especially when it came to Nick's medical needs. We had no idea how to raise a child without limbs, and neither did most of the doctors we encountered. Even a procedure as simple as taking a blood sample becomes much more complex and dangerous when the patient has no limbs.

Whenever blood tests had to be done on Nick, there was considerable debate on how to go about this. Some nurses would prick the toe on his little foot. Others wanted to tap his jugular vein, which can be dangerous. Dushka often had to get aggressive and play her registered-nurse card because she thought caregivers were winging it while treating our son.

Nick's body does not have the same cooling system as the typical patient who shows up in a physician's office or operating room. Most of us release a high percentage of our body heat through our arms and legs. With only a torso, Nick has far less skin surface, and as a result he can become dangerously overheated in a very brief period. Doctors and nurses have not always taken that into consideration.

This was a major concern when Nick was a baby and couldn't speak for himself. Nurses typically swaddle infants to make them feel cozy and warm. Nick was not swaddle-friendly. He'd practically glow red from a high body temperature. Heat rash has always been a problem for him too.

Dushka had to remain vigilant when doctors or nurses treated Nick, constantly warning them that covering him with bedding, wrapping him in blankets, or putting him under hot lights could kill him. Nick's self-roasting tendencies gave rise to a family joke: "When Nicky's cold, the ducks must be freezing."

PARENT ADVOCATES

They say there is healing power in laughter, and thank goodness for that because, as anyone with a disabled or special-needs child knows, medical issues are a serious concern as well as a major expense. Our children typically need advanced and specialized medical care, and they spend more time in hospitals, emergency rooms, and physical and psychological therapy clinics than most kids. In addition, they often need full- or part-time caregivers and expensive medical equipment such as custom wheelchairs, prosthetics, special beds, accessibility ramps, lifts, special baths and showers, and other items.

Psychologists say that access to affordable and competent medical care is critical in order for families with disabled children to attain some semblance of normalcy in their lives. Many families, including ours, have relocated at least once and sometimes more in search of the best doctors, hospitals, clinics, and treatment for their children.

Nick had continuing issues with high body temperatures, heat rashes, urinary infections, and respiratory issues as a child. Dushka felt the rainy and often changing weather of Melbourne might be a factor. When he was around ten years old, Dushka and I concluded that a warmer climate might be beneficial for him. That summer we took a four-week vacation and went to Brisbane, which is more than one thousand miles to the northeast and enjoys a more consistent subtropical climate.

We made this move even though we'd also been considering an even bigger move—to the balmy climate of California in the United States. We had family near Los Angeles who'd been urging us to try life there. We'd given it serious thought because we'd been told the United States was more advanced in its acceptance of disabled people. We thought medical care might be better there too. We had actually applied for my work visa in the United States a couple of years before we moved to Brisbane, but the process of getting it took so long we'd nearly given up. Then, shortly after we'd moved to Brisbane, the three-year permit came through. Dushka could not get her work permit due to the difference in nursing requirements.

We headed to the United States in 1992, but we quickly came to regret our decision. We loved California for its weather and beauty, but it was an expensive place to live on just one salary. We also discovered that the American health-care system, with its private insurance, was much more expensive and not nearly as generous as Australia's socialized system.

It was perhaps unfair to move our children to California so soon after they'd adjusted to Brisbane. They found it more difficult to adapt to California and an entirely different country and school system. Just three months after moving to the United States, Dushka and I decided to return to Australia, partly because our American attorney had told us that we faced a lengthy process to obtain a permanent United States residency permit, and we feared it might never happen. So we moved back to our adopted homeland, where we were on more familiar terrain and found it easier to navigate the educational and medical systems.

HEALTH AND WELL-BEING

Dushka and I are grateful that Nick's medical challenges have been limited mostly to dealing with his lack of limbs and a few other issues related to that. He proved to be an otherwise healthy and durable child. Australia's healthcare system is socialized to a large degree, and while we certainly had some medical bills over the years, they probably were not anywhere near what they might have been in the United States. We also benefitted from the assistance of several organizations that came to Nick's aid as he was growing up.

We often tell other parents that they will need to stand up and serve as aggressive advocates for their children because no one cares as much about their kids as parents do. We were lucky to have a head start because of Dushka's nursing experience, but we still had to educate ourselves and stand by Nick during all his medical procedures. There were a few times when well-meaning medical professionals could have caused serious harm to our son if Dushka had not been there to intervene and guide them.

Parents cannot afford to simply hand their children over to doctors and therapists and leave their treatment to the experts. We also recommend that parents with special-needs kids become well versed on all laws dealing with government health-care support and the rights of those with disabilities and special needs. It is critical that you know the right questions to ask of your child's health-care providers, medical team, and therapists. You should educate yourself about the exact nature of your child's disability and what treatments are most effective.

Because Nick's disability is rare, we didn't have many resources such as support groups, parent organizations, and online forums and websites to help us, but there are certainly many available for other parents whose kids have more common challenges. We also did not have access to the Internet and the world of information it provides.

We found it wise to keep detailed notes, medical records, and time lines of Nick's treatments, prescription drugs, allergies, illnesses, medical procedures, and all other medical matters. You can't rely on your physician to keep these records for you because records can be lost or destroyed.

Finally we recommend that parents work to form alliances and relationships with their medical caregivers because the more they know your child as an individual who is loved, the better they will treat him or her. There is an art to this, and it can be difficult to maintain good relations with all those who treat your child, but we've found that taking time to build personal bonds can enhance the quality of care your child receives.

Parents of disabled and special-needs children often have to make difficult decisions that affect their children's health and quality of life. Many times we were torn when doctors recommended procedures that might benefit Nick's long-term health while adversely impacting his ability to enjoy the active life that was part of his outgoing nature. Sometimes his doctors did not agree with our decisions. We learned to listen to all they had to say and then do what we believed was best for our son's overall quality of life. In some cases, we also had to educate doctors and constantly remind them that some of their standard practices for "normal" patients were not safe for our son.

A HANDY FOOT

Dushka is normally a gentle, charming woman, but she sometimes had to become Nick's Ninja Mom when those providing him with medical care failed to pay attention. This proved to be the case early on when his doctors endeavored to help Nick by operating on one of his greatest physical assets, his larger foot.

Unlike the smaller foot on his right side, Nick's left foot has both a bone and muscle tissue that allows him to manipulate it. At birth it resembled a foot with two large toes fused together. Our hope was that if doctors could separate the toes, Nick might be able to manipulate them both, which would allow him to grasp things with his foot. We thought he might be able to then use the foot to hold a pen and write and do other tasks that are normally done with hands and fingers.

We had seen videos of a girl in England who had no arms but could use her feet to do many things for herself, including cooking dinner, writing, and painting. We were inspired by her ability to adapt to using her feet. After consulting with orthopedic and plastic surgeons, we decided to let them operate on Nick's foot when he was about four years old. We wanted to do anything we could to help our son be as self-sufficient as possible.

When Nick was being prepared for surgery, Dushka reminded the medical team repeatedly that his body temperature could elevate dangerously under bright lights and bed covers. She also mentioned that she'd heard of another child without limbs who had experienced this during an operation and was left with brain damage after suffering a seizure. Even though the doctors knew Dushka was a nurse, they did not pay adequate attention to what she told them.

While they were able to separate Nick's toes during the operation, they nearly overbaked the rest of him. He came out of the operating room soaked with sweat and with a soaring body temperature. They frantically worked to cool him down with buckets of ice before he had a seizure. They also incurred Dushka's wrath for failing to listen to her. From that point on, we always made sure Nick's doctors and nurses had a full understanding of his tendency to self-cook.

GOOD FOOTING

As it turned out, the operation wasn't as successful as we hoped it would be. While the surgeons did free up the two toes, they can't be moved independently of each other, which would have made them more useful to Nick. Eventually, however, he was able to make very good use of the larger foot as it is. He can grasp a pen with it, although often he prefers just to hold the pen in his mouth and write with it that way. He does use the toes for typing and, amazingly, he can peck away at the rate of forty words a minute on his laptop.

As a child, Michelle nicknamed her brother's foot "Nick's little chicken leg" because she thought it resembled a drumstick. He often makes jokes about it, but his ability to manipulate that foot has become one of his biggest assets. He uses it to type, dial a phone, scroll on a tablet, guide a joystick on his wheelchair, and play video games—among other things.

While most people enjoy the convenience of smartphones and their many applications, for our son they are a great gift because they allow him to do so many things that would otherwise be difficult or impossible. This single device allows him to easily talk on the telephone, send e-mails and text messages, play music, watch videos and movies, play games, check his calendar, record sermons and memos, and keep up with the weather and world events.

Before smartphones, most of us could plan a trip by picking up a map, unfolding it, and reading it. Try doing that without any arms or hands! The first cell phones were much bigger, which made it easier for Nick to dial but posed other problems. People couldn't hear him and he couldn't hear them if he left the phone near his foot, so he had to figure out how to dial with his toe and then get the phone closer to his mouth and ears.

Nick's solution was his own version of the flip phone. He practiced for hours dialing the cell phone and then quickly flipping it onto his shoulder. His goal was to catch it between his chin and his collarbone and then hold it there while he conversed. It took him many hours and no little pain. I kept imagining his doctor asking him if all the bruises on his face were from a beating and Nick responding, "Yes, I was attacked by my cell phone." Then again, I'm sure his cell phones took a beating while he was learning to catch them. I don't want to know how many were destroyed during his practice sessions.

THE HUMAN TORPEDO

Nick's ability to manipulate his left foot and to put it to ingenious uses even as a toddler proved to be a blessing in many ways. Dushka and I were surprised and delighted when he was able to stand and walk by using the little foot for leverage, but we were also concerned about the toll it could take on his body over time.

The flesh on the bottom of his thighs wasn't meant to be in constant contact with the floor, pavement, or rough surfaces. When Nick first began moving about on his own, we had to treat the skin down there with moisturizers and balm because it would crack and become tender. It did toughen up eventually, like the soles of our feet do, but we were worried about another potential side effect of Nick's mobility.

Shortly after his birth, doctors told us that Nick had scoliosis, or curvature of the spine, that would likely grow worse as he aged. They advised that the less stress he put on his back, the better. Our son's spinal problems are related to his lack of arms and legs. Normally our limbs help keep our spine straight and in place by distributing our weight evenly. Nick's strong reliance on his left foot for leverage and balance made him tilt his body to that side most of the time, which put additional pressure on his spine and caused his rib cage to rotate slightly. This was further aggravated when he moved about with slight hops, which compacted his spine.

Some of the specialists we consulted suggested putting an iron rod in his back to support the spine, but the downside was that Nick would have very limited movement. Our son is not one to sit still very long, nor is he a couch potato. He has always been extremely active. Friends have dubbed him the "human torpedo" for the way he throws his body around, whether it's diving into a pool or launching himself back and forth over the seats of an SUV as it cruises along the highway. My wife and I were aware by this time that medicine isn't always an exact science. Doctors can make projections and predictions, but with something like scoliosis, there was no accurate way to predict how it would affect Nick in adulthood. We learned that surgeons were often eager to operate on Nick because they saw him as an interesting challenge. The thought of them opening up his back and placing a metal rod in it was disturbing, especially because Nick truly enjoyed being out and about and active with his family and friends.

Dushka and I told the doctors we did not want to constrain Nick. Our goal was to give him even greater mobility if possible, so when he was about two years old, we began searching for a wheelchair that our active son could control. In addition to the added mobility, we thought a wheelchair would elevate Nick so he could be at the same eye level as other children, and with seat belts and padding, it would also help support and hold steady his delicate spine.

We were eager to get him into a wheelchair as soon as possible to save wear and tear on his body. Of course, finding a wheelchair that suited Nick was an issue. Australia's health-care system was quite generous in its benefits, but it provided only standard nonmotorized wheelchairs, which our son was not able to operate.

Nick was about two and a half years old when we learned of an electric wheelchair developed in England. This chair had a joystick control, like a video game, that made it possible for him to operate it with his larger foot. Aptly named the Comet, it was rounded like a barrel with wheels. It was not a thing of beauty, but Nick loved it because it gave him greater freedom to roam about without so much wear and tear on his body.

Dushka and I especially liked that the seat was designed to hold a child firmly in place. The custom chair was expensive, but a hospital in Melbourne with a special clinic for patients who lacked limbs offered to provide one to Nick.

RIDING THE LITTLE RED COMET

Strangely, when we told Nick's medical team about it, they were not enthused. His physical therapist and doctors thought he was too young to operate it safely. Nick was adamant that he could do it, and by that time, we were much more inclined to side with our son. Finally the medical team came around and gave their okay.

The manufacturer sent the wheelchair along with a technician who taught Nick how to operate it. Everyone was astounded at how quickly he learned to zip around in it. Since it was rounded, low to the ground, and bright red in color, we nicknamed it the Little Red Comet, and Nick seemed to take that to heart. He was soon flying all over the neighborhood in it, once again exceeding all expectations.

The Little Red Comet was the first and most rudimentary in what has proven to be a long line of expensive custom-made wheelchairs for our son. I am not complaining, by the way. Power wheelchairs have enhanced Nick's quality of life to an incredible degree. They've enabled him to travel and speak around the world. As the technology has evolved, he's found power wheelchairs that lower all the way to the ground so he can just hop aboard and then raise himself to be eye to eye with his friends and audiences.

In fact, one of the most joyous memories I have of Nick and Kanae's wedding is when they rolled onto the dance floor with Kanae in her bridal gown riding on his wheelchair. Then they performed a beautiful dance together, moving to the music. It was a wonderful moment that left everyone teary eyed.

THE MATRIMONY MOBILE

Most people did not realize that the wheelchair was Nick's "wedding special," designed specifically for this milestone event. The designer completed it just in time for the wedding, which is a good thing because Nick's previous model had been worn out and was hardly operational.

Nick specified to the builder that he wanted to be at a comfortable height for dancing with his bride at their wedding. The wedding special was like the Porsche of wheelchairs because it was also very fast and highly maneuverable. In fact, after the wedding Kanae told us that the wheelchair was so fast and maneuverable that Nick nearly sent her flying off the back when they came swooping into the wedding reception.

The wheelchair technology has evolved to an incredible degree, and so has the cost. Some of them actually use the same motors as those that run the windshield wiper blades on cars. Newer models come with their own apps for smartphones. Nearly all of Nick's had to be custom made to accommodate for his lack of limbs and his scoliosis, not to mention his world travels and his daredevil driving style.

The only model that was not custom made for Nick was a wheelchair he had in elementary school. Called the YoYo, it was made in New Zealand and Australia. This was his second wheelchair. It too could be lowered so he could just hop in and then raise himself to the same height as his classmates. It was much lighter and smaller in size, which was better for transporting it in the van. In hindsight, I should have bought two or three of them because they were reasonably priced and suited Nick well, but the business shut down a few years later.

Our son can't shake hands or give arm hugs, so his method for engaging with people is to make eye contact. Even as a child, he was so good at this that adults often remarked about his ability to communicate through his eyes. It was very important to him, then, to have wheelchairs that brought him up to a normal height so that he wasn't always looking up to those around him.

As he was growing up, and even as an adult, Nick has tried to figure out what his height would be if he had legs. He estimates that he would have been nearly six feet tall as an adult. He likes his chair positioned to put him around that height, especially when he is with Kanae, which is understandable.

Nick became quite skilled at driving his motorized chairs at a very young age. He had a few crashes and mishaps over the years, but he mostly wore out his wheelchairs or outgrew them. I think he went through five or six of them before he hit the age of twenty-one. We were fortunate in that most were paid for through donations from organizations, including the Lions Club.

WHEELING ROUND THE WORLD

Nick now usually pays for his own wheelchairs, and it is no small expense because he has lighter but durable models that are suitable for transportation on airplanes for his global travels. He keeps more substantial wheelchairs at home for getting around the house and around town, often with his son and maybe even his wife on board. The mobility that a motorized wheelchair provides has changed his life, and that makes Nick highly sympathetic to other disabled people who can't afford one.

Over the years, he has supported the efforts of his mentor, Joni Eareckson Tada, whose nonprofit Wheels for the World ministry has donated thousands of wheelchairs to disabled people around the world. And on at least one occasion, my son simply hopped out of his own customized wheelchair and gave it to someone who seemed to need it more.

This occurred on the final leg of nearly six months of travel in 2013. Nick, who was road weary to the point of exhaustion, was speaking in Columbia, South America, when he saw a limbless teen with one small foot. The boy was in a battered manual wheelchair. Nick was compelled to learn more about this young man. Through an interpreter, the boy said he lived in a small village but attended school in the city an hour away. Every day he was carried an hour to the bus stop so he could take the bus into town. After class, he made the hour-long trip back to his home. He told Nick that he wanted to continue his studies, but his lack of mobility had become a major concern.

Maybe it was because the teen's disabilities were very similar to Nick's. Maybe it was because it was almost Christmastime. But mostly, as Nick later said, "I felt God asking me to do something, to step outside my own frustrations and focus on the needs in front of me."

Nick initiated a wheelchair swap, and the Columbian teen certainly got the better part of the deal. In fact, Nick later sweetened the deal and threw in a generator for the teen and his family after learning that the boy's town had no electricity, which would be needed to charge the battery-powered wheelchair. "Never have I felt God move through me in that way," Nick said.

Once again our son exceeded all expectations and made his parents proud. By the way, Nick finished the final leg of that tour riding about in the Columbian teen's wheelchair because he didn't have a battery-powered backup on the trip.

HEAVY LIFTING

As Nick grew, his wheelchairs became more sophisticated and heavier. His current model is more than 180 pounds, without Nick on board. The placement of the motor and batteries is important because they have to balance out the weight of the person in the chair. I was constantly telling Nick to slow down or be careful as he rolled up and down hills or ramps as a boy because I feared he'd fall over backward or hit something and crash forward. My warnings annoyed him, I'm sure, but that's what parents do, right?

As anyone who needs a wheelchair knows, the cost of the chair itself is just the beginning. Most people need a vehicle big enough to haul the chair around, and a way to get the chair into that vehicle.

During Nick's speaking events in Serbia in 2012, he was visiting with professional tennis player Novak Djokovic and his family at Novak's restaurant. Late at night when he was to be dropped off at the hotel, there was no adequate-size taxi to transport his wheelchair. Novak's father, who lived nearby, went home, picked up his vehicle, and kindly drove Nick and the wheelchair to the hotel.

Power wheelchairs are always a challenge to transport because of their weight. We have had both hydraulic lifts mounted on vans and portable ramps for SUVs. The portable ramps are less expensive and more practical in many ways, but they require careful use. The hydraulic lifts are bulky and costly, though easier to use.

When Nick was about six years old, we had a big van with a custom hoist that swiveled out from the car, dropped to the ground, and then reversed the process to load Nick into the van while still in his wheelchair. This was a handy setup that connected to the battery of the car and was fully automated. We had to make sure Nick and his chair were both secured before we moved the hoist, however. On one occasion, our son and his wheelchair went spilling out of the hoist in our driveway, and Nick took a pretty good blow to his chin. It left a scar. Nick has been known to blame the scar on a close call in a sword duel.

ACCESSIBLE LIVING

Whenever we've built or shopped for homes, we've looked for open plans with either no hallways or very wide ones. Wide doors were also a priority to allow access for Nick's wheelchairs. We also tried to have easy access bathroom showers, and we devised low racks in them so Nick could get soap and shampoo by stepping on a foot pump.

The house we built in Melbourne next to the school he was going to attend in Keilor Downs was designed for Nick's needs as we perceived them at the time, including heated floors because he spent so much time down there in the chilly weather. We stayed in that house until Nick was nine years old. We then moved to Brisbane and built a house there with a slightly different setup.

We'd been displeased with the efficiency of the floor-heating system in an ever-changing climate. The system took nearly twenty-four hours to warm the slab under the flooring, and often by that time the weather would change and it would not be comfortable for Nick. Then the slab needed another half day or more to cool, so we had to open windows to make it more comfortable.

As Nick grew, he was able to move about more on his own, either hopping about or using his adjustable chair to remain off the floor. He could also hop into the shower so we no longer needed a customized entrance. In Brisbane, which has a subtropical climate, we had little need of a heater or furnace. We used reverse-cycle air conditioners mostly for cooling in summertime, but also for heating when we needed to take some chill out on some winter nights and mornings.

LIFE WITH LIMBS?

Technological advancements and greater access have been beneficial, but Nick hasn't abandoned his dream of a miracle. He still keeps a pair of shoes in his closet in case God decides one day to provide him with arms and legs. Over the years, many people have suggested that Nick should try man-made limbs while waiting for God to answer his prayers. This option has become more intriguing in recent years as science and technology have advanced significantly in the manufacturing of prosthetic limbs.

Dushka and I had once thought that artificial arms and legs might be a boon to our son, but our early experiences in this arena didn't turn out like we'd hoped. When Nick was four and a half years old, the local Lions Club of Melbourne and Wholesale Produce Market began a nationwide campaign to fund artificial limbs for him. Their efforts resulted in the creation of a trust fund to finance this expensive proposition.

Before we knew it, the Lions Club had arranged for Nick, accompanied by Dushka and our younger son, Aaron, to travel from Australia to a highly regarded clinic in Toronto, Canada. Air Canada provided their air travel at no charge. They were invited to stay with a family in Toronto during the six-week visit. I could not go because at that time I was working as a cost accountant and going to university to complete my business degree so I could get a better-paying job.

Our interest in prosthetics had increased after we'd learned of an older lady, a Thalidomide victim, who'd received myoelectric arms, which use electrodes to capture the small electrical signals generated by muscles when they contract. The artificial arms can be programmed to respond to electronic signals. They can also be used to open and close a prosthetic hand on the artificial arms.

We weren't sure this would work for Nick because his arm sockets are empty, so attaching prosthesis seemed like a difficult matter. Still, we thought it was worth a visit to see what the team in Toronto might figure out for him. Nick was very excited at the prospect.

The name of the Toronto clinic was the Hugh MacMillan Rehabilitation Centre (now known as the Holland Bloorview Kids Rehabilitation Hospital). Dushka found it to be a world-class facility with a caring and professional staff. She and Aaron spent many long hours in the lab with Nick, the star patient.

The first three weeks were taken up with assessing him, measuring his little body, and applying a plaster cast to make a mold so they could create a custom-fit frame. When Nick wasn't being poked, prodded, or plastered, he and his brother roamed the corridors, making friends and playing with the other children in waiting rooms.

We were delighted that the clinic also provided swimming lessons for Nick, given by an occupational therapist in the center's pool. He had already learned to float, but these sessions gave him greater confidence and better techniques. He took glee in creating his own little whirlpool by spinning himself round and round in the water with his foot.

A DIFFICULT FIT

Sadly there were also a great many frustrations and disappointments in this first experience with prosthetics. The original goal was to fit Nick with state-of-the-art myoelectric arms and hands controlled by muscle contractions and electrodes, but the prosthetic team quickly realized that Nick's unique body was not at all suited for that technology. Since his arms had never formed in any way, there was not enough muscle tissue to work with.

Their plan B was to fit him with the older mechanical model that required Nick to manually operate his artificial arms and hands with switches. The metal frame for the mechanical prosthesis was made of lightweight material, but it was bulky. Once they had fit the arms by mounting them across his shoulders in a molded plastic shell with artificial arms and hands attached, they worked for many hours to teach him how to operate the switches.

Dushka said it was an emotional experience watching Nick's determined struggle to manipulate the arms and hands. He failed time and again, but never once did he give in to frustration. Our son was very patient and persevered in learning to perform very complex movements to complete tasks with the clunky mechanical arms and hands.

Nick had to twist his torso in awkward ways to position the arms and hands correctly, but he eventually learned to grip items, including spoons and cups, so that he could pick them up, move them to his mouth, and feed himself.

Dushka found it quite surreal to see little Nick sitting in his chair, wearing a shirt, with arms resting, hands clasped. From just a short distance, the flesh-colored plastic limbs were quite realistic looking. She took photographs and sent them to me. For the first time, we had a glimpse of what he would have looked like if he had upper limbs. Wow!

We were grateful to the center's staff and to all the people who made it possible for our son to be fitted and trained to use the artificial limbs. That said, we were disappointed that more advanced prosthesis could not be adapted for him at that point. We also realized it would take a long period of adjustment and practice before Nick felt natural wearing and using the mechanical arms, especially in school.

A Fair Go

When Dushka and the boys returned home, we let Nick know how proud we were that he had tried so hard and learned to use the mechanical limbs. He put them on each day to practice with them, and he became fairly adept at using them. He could pick up his food and bring it to his mouth, scratch his head, and even shake hands. In the first few months, he enjoyed being able to pick up and play with his toys. The artificial hands gave Nick a very strong grip. His little brother, Aaron, learned to stay out of reach because Nick delighted in giving him a squeeze or a pinch.

The overall experience, however, wasn't so good. Though Nick tried for more than a year to use the mechanical prosthesis, there were several reasons why this first experience ultimately failed. No matter how often he wore them and practiced using them, there was no escaping the fact that this particular model was very uncomfortable and awkward for our small boy to wear for any length of time.

Nick complained that wearing the prosthesis hurt his back. This was a major concern to us due to his scoliosis and the vulnerability of his spine. The metal frame covered in hard plastic also caused Nick's body to heat up, and that was another serious issue because if his body temperature ran too high, he developed a rash and felt uncomfortable and perspired greatly.

Finally there was the fact that this particular prosthetic device did not do much to improve our son's quality of life. In many ways, using it was more difficult. Nick had already figured out ways to accomplish most tasks, and his methods usually were simpler and easier for him and felt more natural.

We appreciated everyone's efforts on Nick's behalf, but after more than a year of watching him struggle with the prosthesis, it was not a difficult decision to put it in storage and let him just go back to being natural.

He gave it a fair go. Many people had suggested that we explore this option, and we're glad we did. We also took into consideration the fact that Nick would have to be refitted at least every couple of years as he grew. Not only would that have been expensive, it also would have put him through many more hours in clinics being assessed, poked, and prodded.

There were times during the Toronto experience, and many times over the years at other hospitals and clinics, when Dushka and I felt enough is enough. It seemed invasive, impersonal, and sometimes exploitive. Sometimes we'd get no helpful feedback at all. Watching our child bravely struggle to please his doctors and parents sometimes left us wondering if the effort was worth the reward. Dushka's mother-bear instincts were always to protect Nick's quality of life and his self-esteem. Our feeling was that he had more than enough challenges in life without subjecting him to unnecessary stress and strain.

PROBING AND PRICKING

We discovered over the years that because a child born without limbs is fairly rare, there were physicians and researchers who were just curious or felt it would be a feather in their cap to examine Nick for their studies and papers. Some requested that we bring Nick to medical conferences; others asked us to send his x-rays. We reached a point where we decided not to cooperate unless there was some tangible benefit to Nick or a dramatic new development in technology or medical procedures. Of course Nick is now an adult, and these decisions and challenges rest with him.

Over the years we considered trying more advanced artificial limbs, but we always decided his quality of life would not be significantly improved. Nick may want to try again one day because there certainly have been dramatic advances. Some researchers are predicting that surgeons will be able to transplant entire limbs within a few years. That opens up all sorts of interesting possibilities.

Also, recent wars around the world have resulted in an astounding number of amputations. As a result, the United States government has become a major investor in the development of artificial limbs. The technology has advanced rapidly and now includes prosthesis that are lightweight and much closer to functioning like real limbs. In addition, there are now robotic exoskeletons that fit over the body or parts of the body, much like what is worn by the fictional character Iron Man.

These new technologies and medical advances are fascinating, but there is also the fact that Nick has made an incredible life for himself, just as he is. He may decide to leave well enough alone.

From my point of view as his father, I care only that he has a good quality of life and that he is surrounded by people who love him and care for him and want only the best for him. I don't need Iron Nick or RoboNick. I'm very happy with just plain Nick, who is an incredible child of God and a blessing to us all.

TAKEAWAY THOUGHTS

- Become the medical expert on your child's health and needs, and be prepared to fight for whatever is best for his or her long-term well-being. No one will care as much as you do.
- Know the laws governing the health-care rights of disabled and special-needs kids in your community, state, and country so that you can be an effective advocate.
- Prepare for every doctor, therapist, and hospital visit so that you know the right questions to ask.

- Keep detailed medical records and notes on your smartphone, laptop, and home computer for emergencies. Your records should include all surgeries, treatments for illnesses, injuries, and allergies, as well as all prescription and nonprescription drugs. Do not ever trust that your physician or emergency-room doctor is aware of your child's entire medical history.

- Make the most of all medical and health resources, including support groups relevant to your child's needs, online forums, websites, and expert blogs. Be cautious about information on the Internet, however, and never follow advice unless your child's physician approves it or you've checked it out thoroughly with other experts and other parents.

- Do your best to maintain good relationships with your child's doctors, nurses, office and hospital staff, therapists, and caregivers while letting them know you will advocate strongly for the best treatment for your child.

Six

Brothers and Sisters

Give the Siblings All They Need Too

Before Nick's birth, Dushka and I had planned on having more than one child. Afterward we weren't so sure it was a good idea. We consulted with doctors, who assured us it was extremely unlikely we would have another child with similar physical disabilities.

Still, we wondered if the genetic mutation thought to cause Nick's lack of limbs was related to something in the environment that could affect any other children we might have. Dushka even fretted that Nick's birth defects might somehow be related to the x-rays she'd been exposed to while working in hospitals. We were bothered by the fact that we had no solid, undeniable cause for our first child's disability.

Dushka and I had many discussions on whether we should have more children and run the risk. There are those who say having children is a selfish act done out of ego. We don't believe that. We believe it is an expression of love. The Bible says children are a blessing from God. Nick has certainly been that, but at the time we were concerned about our ability to care for another child with disabilities while also giving Nick all he needed for a good life.

This was a difficult decision and one I'm sure many parents have to make if they already are caring for a special-needs child. It's also a very personal matter affected by a wide array of circumstances, so I can't offer general advice to other parents. Dushka and I made the decision to try to have another child based on our doctors' assurances.

We also took into consideration that Nick had proven to be much less of a burden than we had originally feared. He had already made it quite clear to us that he was an active, intelligent, and determined little fellow. Nick didn't need constant supervision. That's not the case with more seriously disabled or special-needs kids who have to be monitored around the clock. Dushka and I might have made a different decision if our son required substantially more care because of mental disabilities or more crippling physical disabilities. We were grateful Nick was able to do so much on his own even without limbs. One of our considerations in deciding to have at least one more child was the fact that we thought Nick would benefit from having siblings who accepted him and loved him unconditionally.

Okay, I'll admit there was another factor. Dushka wanted to have a daughter along with our son. Once again, our plans didn't quite work out exactly as we'd hoped in that one regard. Nick was not quite two years old when Dushka became pregnant again. Everyone was happy for us. If any friends or family members had concerns, they didn't share them.

We did ask our doctor to check and recheck the sonograms very thoroughly during this pregnancy. He said this child was another boy, but his limbs were visible and appeared to be normal. We were just fine with another boy. We thought another son would give Nick a sturdy playmate if all went well, and we could always try for a girl later.

BROTHERLY LOVE

Even with our doctors' assurances, we still were relieved when our second son, Aaron, was born without disabilities. We couldn't help but do a quick check on this baby to make sure all limbs and fingers and toes were present and accounted for. With this child, Dushka had a much less stressful birthing experience, and there was a great deal of celebrating.

We named our second son after the Bible's Aaron, who served as a source of support for his brother, Moses, although in their case, Aaron was the older of the two brothers. The Bible tells us that Moses and Aaron stood side by side against the Pharaoh throughout all the plagues and the march out of Egypt. We liked that thought, and it has proven true of our two sons, who have supported each other through good times and bad. The Bible also describes Aaron as the designated spokesperson for Moses. You may recall in the previous chapter, I noted that it was Aaron who came to me with the warning that Nick was contemplating suicide before his twenty-first birthday. We had named him well, apparently.

Scripture offers accounts of the brothers having many adventures together, and that would be true of Nick and Aaron as well. Aaron quickly grew bigger than Nick, and we had to keep an eye on him because he liked to try to pick up his older brother and move him around. Nick wasn't thrilled with that, and he'd make his displeasure known by biting Aaron or pinching him with his chin or his left foot when they were little. The little brother learned to stay out of range.

I had to admire Nick's agility even at a young age. Whenever Aaron would try to snatch one of his toys away, Nick was quite adept at using his body to block him out, like a soccer player protecting the ball from an opponent. Most of the time, they got along fine.

There is a different dynamic, obviously, when a disabled child is not the eldest in the family. I've heard other parents say that their older kids had trouble adjusting to a younger sibling with disabilities because the family's life was so dramatically altered.

We didn't have that problem because our two younger kids grew up with

Nick always there. They naturally accepted him as he was, and they really didn't have any questions about why he was different from them until they reached school age. Aaron and, later, Michelle thought nothing of stepping in to help Nick if they saw he needed something. They were simply following what they'd seen Dushka and me do for him.

Mealtimes were interesting when they were little because everyone sort of chipped in to make sure Nick had what he needed. The other kids thought nothing of cutting up his food, putting straws in his drinks, and even feeding him with a spoon or fork. No one was required or designated to feed or assist Nick at family meals. We just jumped in when he needed something. This was such a natural thing for us that when the kids would have friends over, they'd join in too, thinking nothing of feeding Nick as they all chatted and teased each other.

WRONG ROLES

Problems can arise if the disabled child dominates siblings, becomes overly reliant on them, or demands that they serve his needs, treating them like caregivers or servants rather than respecting their roles as brothers and sisters. We were careful to make sure Nick didn't dominate Aaron's time when they were young. He was good about not doing that as they grew older, but early on we had to set some ground rules because Nick sometimes became a bit bossy.

When a young sibling is forced to take on responsibilities for a disabled child that should belong to the mother or father, there is a chance it can diminish the quality of the sibling's childhood experiences. Psychologists call this parentification, and they say it can stunt the emotional growth of siblings.

Dushka and I learned to be vigilant on this and several other fronts when it came to the relationship between Nick and Aaron and our third child, Michelle, our beautiful daughter who was born with no disabilities two and a half years after Aaron. Dushka was delighted to have another female in the house, and of course I was too. Michelle proved to be an equal match for her brothers and, in fact, they both doted on her. The relationships between siblings are said to be among the most complicated, impassioned, and enduring of any we form. When one of them is a special-needs child, the others can be affected in both positive and negative ways. Dushka and I were well aware of that, and we were also aware that we could have an impact on which way it went for our kids.

We'd heard of siblings who grew up with resentment or who felt burdened or embarrassed by a disabled child in the family. In some cases, siblings of disabled kids have felt guilty because they were normal or healthy and were spared any disabilities. Other siblings may feel they have to be perfect super-achievers who never do any wrong, excel in everything they do, and thus do not place any additional stress on their parents.

We certainly did not want any of those negative feelings or pressures to affect our children and their relationships with each other. To help them form positive, lasting, and loving bonds, we did our best to provide Aaron and Michelle with a full understanding of Nick's disabilities, their origins, and what he could and could not do for himself. We also tried to give our other two kids equal time and attention so they did not feel neglected or less important to us than Nick.

The Bible's Jacob blundered badly when he showed favoritism to his youngest son, Joseph, and provided him with that special coat of many colors. Parents can easily fall into the trap of favoring and spoiling the youngest child, sometimes because the other kids have worn them out and they have no will or energy left.

Children first learn the values of fairness, equality, and justice from their parents, and we did our best to be good role models for them. We also taught them that in the Bible the apostle James admonished Christians not to be partial in their treatment of others and not to dislike or look down upon the poor or underprivileged.

SETTING BOUNDARIES

There was another side to the issue of fairness. We didn't want Nick to take unfair advantage of his siblings' giving nature. There is sometimes a tendency among the parents of disabled children to spoil them rather than discipline them. I understand the reason. A child born with disabilities comes into the world with a greater burden than most.

Parents may feel a child with a disability deserves a break or more leniency. That philosophy may spring from good intentions, but it will likely result in problems down the road. This approach could make the life of the disabled child more difficult. Every child needs boundaries.

A disabled child who grows up without boundaries may lack discipline, social skills, or emotional intelligence as an adult. Men and women with disabilities can live independent lives, but often they rely on the kindness of others to ease their burdens. No one wants to help a selfish, demanding, controlling, or self-centered person—disabled or not.

There are positive methods for disciplining children that include helping them understand what is inappropriate behavior and giving them guidance on what is appropriate as an alternative: "Biting your brother if he takes your toy is not okay. If he won't give it to you, come to me or find something else to play with. Do you understand?"

The discipline and punishment should fit the crime, and it should be consistent so that your child learns right and wrong as well as respect for others. If the bad behavior intensifies, parents will likely need to make the punishment more severe by removing the child from others, taking away privileges, and canceling favorite activities until proper behavior returns.

Nick has always had a strong personality, which includes a strong will and tons of determination, so as a child he needed plenty of guidance. He had to learn the limits and abide by rules. Like most kids, he preferred playing video games and skateboarding to doing his homework or household chores. We had very tightly enforced schedules for homework and housework as well as for playtime.

FINDING BALANCE

Our guiding rule was the Golden Rule, cited by Jesus: "Do to others what you would have them do to you" and "Love your neighbor as yourself." Nick was not a mean child in any way, but he sometimes expected others to do what he wanted them to do, whether or not it was what they wanted to do. If we noticed that Nick was demanding too much of Aaron or bossing him around, we intervened. As the boys grew together, we had to remind Nick from time to time that Aaron was not his servant and that if he needed help, he should ask for it politely and graciously. I regard this as a learning experience for both the boys.

Older brothers and sisters often try to rule over their younger siblings. The unique aspect with a disabled sibling is that Aaron might have felt more compelled to follow Nick's commands—or guilty for not complying—because there were some things Nick could not do for himself. We didn't want Nick to abuse that or to dominate his little brother's time. The broader lesson we provided Nick was that he should not feel entitled to the assistance of others. Instead, he should be humble and grateful to those who step up and help him, whether it's his siblings, teachers' aides, classmates, friends, or professional caregivers.

We expected Aaron to love his brother and to be helpful to him, but we assured our second son that he didn't have to do everything Nick demanded of him. It was a delicate balance to establish. We also feared that Nick would become too dependent on Aaron to do things for him. This played out when Aaron was in his early teens and had a friend stay overnight. They got up in the morning after Dushka and I had left to run errands, so big brother Nick cheerfully took charge.

"Good morning, mates! Would you like me to make you some breakfast?" he said to Aaron and his guest.

"Sure, Nick," they replied.

"Okay, Aaron. Get the eggs. Get the pan. Break the eggs in the pan, then turn on the stove . . ."

No one expected Nick to cook breakfast, of course, but we all enjoyed the fact that he offered to do it for Aaron and his friend and then without any qualms put Aaron to the task—and his brother stepped up without objection!

This is often the dynamic of disabled children and their siblings, and as long as it's a mutually beneficial, loving, and accepted relationship, there is no problem. As they grew older, Aaron made a stand for his independence, which we expected and actually welcomed. We wanted him to have his own identity beyond being Nick's brother.

The same is true of our daughter, Michelle, now a registered nurse who also has a degree in music production. Nick gave her rides on his wheelchair in their younger days. When our three kids played together, they adapted to Nick's disabilities quite naturally. There were just a few minor gripes that he had an unfair advantage when playing hide-and-seek because he could fit into places no one else could—including dresser drawers and laundry baskets.

BROTHER-BOARDING

Michelle spent more time playing with her female cousins and schoolmates than with her rough-and-tumble brothers. Still, she could hold her own when they were together. She was a bit of a tomboy and didn't let anyone push her around. In fact, she sometimes kept her older brother underfoot—and underwater at the same time.

Nick and Aaron would play in the surf all day long. Nick lay on a boogie board and Aaron towed him through the surf, sometimes whipping him about until Nick went flying into the water. It wasn't until recently that we learned one of Michelle's favorite childhood water sports was "Nick-surfing."

Nick has always loved swimming because he has more mobility in the water than on land. Our other kids wore inflatable floaties on their arms to keep them buoyant. Nick couldn't do that, but he was like one big floatie himself. Without the weight of arms and legs, he can float and paddle around for hours simply by keeping a little bit of air in his lungs.

Nick's book *Unstoppable* reflects his fierce determination in the title, but he's also rather unsinkable because there is always some measure of air in our lungs. This is where Michelle's Nick-surfing originated. One of Nick's boyhood games was to see how long he could hold his breath underwater (believe me, we monitored this closely after he told us of his suicide attempt). Nick had a bit of a problem staying down for the count in the swimming pool, however, because he'd keep popping up to the surface. His solution was to swim to the bottom of the shallow section and have his delighted little sister stand on his back during his countdown.

Michelle tried to stay on board her brother until he kicked his left foot to indicate he wanted to surface. I'm assuming Nick made sure to treat his little sister very well so that she didn't one day decide to surf him beyond his lung capacity.

Nick apparently still enjoys this little game, because not too long ago his wife, Kanae, posted a photo of her standing atop Nick as he rested at the bottom of their pool. They say the best marriages are built on trust, and a man would certainly have to trust his wife to allow her to do that!

THE REEL NICK

Fishing off the coast of Australia or in its lakes and rivers was one of our most enjoyable family pastimes when the kids were growing up, in part because everyone could participate. It didn't matter to the fish on the other end of the line. Nick became the most avid fisherman in the family. We bought him a battery-operated reel so he could retrieve his line simply by pushing a button with his left foot. He could throw out the line and set the hook by holding the pole between his chin and shoulder and swinging his body to send it flying.

If Nick hooked something big, we strapped him into a chair, or Michelle and Aaron held on to him as we helped him bring the fish in. Most of the time Nick didn't need our help. He was a very eager fisherman but not always so patient in his younger days. He tended to yank on the line to set the hook before the fish was ready.

If he was fishing from land and hooked something, Nick's usual tactic was to hold on to the pole and hop backward until he brought the fish to shore. On one occasion, he didn't have enough room to do that when he hooked a big fish in the river. They were having quite a battle. The fish was too big to reel in with the automatic reel, so Nick decided to bring in the line by spinning like a top, winding it around himself. He landed the fish, but it took us nearly an hour to untangle Nick and the fishing line. We told Nick he made a better fisherman than a reel.

We taught our children to be generous with each other and never to take each other for granted. They seemed to take our lessons to heart, but that's not to say they were little angels or that they didn't ever bicker. Our kids had the normal sibling clashes, and they had to be reminded from time to time that Dushka and I were running the show.

The other kids were known to play the "Nick card" now and then. Michelle and Aaron staged a minor rebellion when we declared they had to earn their weekly allowances by working around the house. They noted that Nick had not been required to earn his allowance by doing housework. Michelle showed her dramatic side when she pushed this point by announcing, "I wish I'd been born without arms or legs so I wouldn't have to do any cleaning!"

That comment got our attention. We had a little talk with Michelle to give her a fresh perspective on all the challenges her older brother had to deal with because of his disability. Yet we also had to concede that maybe Nick shouldn't be held to a different standard than his siblings when it came to chores.

He'd proven himself capable of holding a fishing rod, swinging a bat, and chipping and putting with golf clubs by holding them between his chin and shoulder. We figured he could swing the vacuum cleaner too. It was a built-in system, so the burden wasn't all that great. Nick wasn't thrilled when we added his name to the household duty roster, but he quickly accepted it and pitched in.

From that point forward, we cut Nick no slack. He was expected to make his bed and keep his room clean just like his siblings. You might think this was asking too much, or at least you may be wondering, *How does someone with no limbs make the bed?* Nick actually took this as a challenge and figured out how to do it. I won't say the neatness of his bed would have passed inspection by a US Marine sergeant, but he actually did a decent job.

Sporting Chances

Dushka and I spent a lot of time encouraging Nick, cheering him on when he accomplished tasks, and tending to his medical needs and his schooling. There were challenges to overcome in many areas of his life. We were always aware, however, that Aaron and Michelle also needed to be focused upon—if not equally, at least as much as possible. We didn't want them to feel neglected or less loved than Nick.

There is a delicate balance to parenting children in any family, of course. When there is a disabled child in the mix, the need to give each child adequate attention becomes a larger challenge. There was no way around the fact that we had to spend more time tending to Nick's medical needs, his education, and his daily care. We compensated for this as best we could by trying to focus on Aaron and Michelle at every opportunity and by encouraging Nick to do the same.

We had to be careful in our approach to equal treatment, especially when we encouraged our two youngest children to participate in activities that Nick simply wasn't capable of doing. We didn't want Nick to feel left out or sad because he couldn't join them, yet we wanted to cheer on the others. When Aaron was about nine, we felt it would be good for him to get involved in sporting activities. We signed him up for the local kids' soccer club. We wanted him to compete with other boys and make friends outside the family so that he formed his own identity and social circles.

At the same time, we knew that seeing his little brother play soccer and make his own friends might cause Nick to feel sad or left out. Nick wasn't usually inclined to self-pity, but he did love soccer and often said he wished he could run on the field with the other boys. When Nick was younger and close to their size, he was pretty hard to beat when playing soccer in our living room with Aaron and their cousins. In that small space, Nick didn't have to move around all that much and his left foot could be a potent weapon for short-range goals. He is also fairly amazing with headshots, and not just in soccer.

There is at least one thrilling video on YouTube that captures Nick putting a basketball into the net with a headshot—and he insists he had to try only a couple of times before he made it. He managed to do this while standing atop a desk in front of an entire gymnasium of people (www.youtube .com/watch?v=v08l3_sebeA).

As it turned out, Nick was a good sport about his brother playing on the local soccer club. Dushka and I knew it wasn't easy for him to stand on the sidelines, and our hearts ached for him, but Nick was very gracious in cheering on Aaron, encouraging him, and, of course, offering big brother's coaching tips.

Sadly, children with disabilities do reach a point when they run up against limitations that separate them from other kids. As a parent you want to stay positive. You encourage your children to do the best they can. You want them to dare to rise above expectations. Yet the fact remains that despite his enthusiasm for athletics, he could not compete in sports on the same level as other children. He has a competitive nature, so that was tough for him to accept and not easy for his parents to watch.

Nick handled it well enough. He did not mope around or feel sorry for himself. He went to the matches and supported Aaron, cheering him on when his little brother did well and won trophies and awards. Dushka and I thought it was a very healthy thing for our other kids to have their time in the limelight too.

DISABILITY BY ASSOCIATION

Social workers, therapists, and psychologists told us in the early days that siblings respond in both positive and negative ways to a brother or sister who is disabled, chronically ill, or has special needs. Some become protective and supportive. Others feel anxiety and even concern that they might contract the disability or illness one day. As they grow older, siblings can experience stress if they worry that they will become responsible for the disabled family member later in life.

Guidelines for parents of disabled children typically say that siblings age five and under don't usually understand the nature of the family member's disabilities, but they are aware of some difference and often will try to assist their sibling. Siblings six to twelve years old are more likely to understand disabilities, but they may worry they are contagious, feel guilty about any negative thoughts toward the disabled sibling, and have conflicting feelings and attitudes ranging from overly affectionate to resentful.

Teenagers generally are better at grasping the complexities of a disabled sibling's condition. They also may ask provocative and probing questions, and it is not unusual for them to feel insecure and embarrassed in front of their friends because of the disabled sibling. Often teens, who have a tendency to be self-absorbed and independent minded, can resent having any responsibilities for a disabled sibling. Yet teens also can feel strongly connected to and empathetic toward disabled siblings.

Those are just general guidelines, of course. Dushka and I always advise parents not to take anything for granted by expecting the other kids to simply "deal with" the sibling who has special needs. Friends and schoolmates can easily disrupt the relationships among your children by taunting, bullying, or shunning them because of the disabled child in the family.

Again, communication is critical. The more time you spend with your children, listening to them and asking them about their lives and their feelings, the better equipped you will be to help them build loving and supportive bonds.

Before Aaron and Michelle began their school years, they lived in a bubble of sorts. Despite Nick's obvious physical disability and the challenges that came with it, we had a fairly normal existence. Dushka and I did our best to give all our kids the attention and love they needed. Nick deserves credit too because he generally did not demand to be the focal point, and he was usually quite an active, engaging, and loving brother. As I've noted before, we were also blessed to have a large extended family of aunts, uncles, and cousins who provided a cocoon of normalcy through their love, support, and acceptance.

As Aaron and Michelle left that family cocoon and entered their school years, we worried about them being vulnerable or stigmatized as Nick's brother and sister. He was small, but Nick's shadow was considerable. Nick became one of the first disabled students to be mainstreamed in Australia's school system, and he became the poster child for that groundbreaking movement. The media sought him out and interviewed him often. He handled it very well, as you might imagine.

By the time Aaron and Michelle entered school, their telegenic brother was a national celebrity in Australia. Both teachers and schoolmates saw them as "Nick's brother" and "Nick's sister." This had both positive and negative implications for them.

Kids can be intentionally cruel, and there was some of that, but more often the hurtful comments were just kids being kids. It was bad enough that Nick had to put up with indiscrete questions about his methods for using the bathroom or whether he had all the essential reproductive organs. His brother and sister were sometimes asked by classmates to report on these same matters on behalf of their older brother.

Kids with special-needs siblings are often subjected to teasing, taunts, bullying, and social isolation. This is so common that psychologists and sociologists have a name for it—disability by association.

There have been many studies and reports on this. Some of the typical remarks aimed at siblings include the following: "Are you going to end up like your brother someday?" "Why don't you have what your brother has?" "Aren't you embarrassed to have a brother like that?" "Your family is weird!"

Fortunately our children experienced very little of that sort of thing as far as I know. Other parents have shared that their disabled child's siblings aren't invited to social gatherings or find that friends are reluctant to come to their homes because of the child with special needs.

One of the goals of mainstreaming is to reduce stigmas and prejudices by allowing other kids to get to know their disabled classmates as individuals. I believe this worked to a large degree for our children, and I'm certain that in the years since Nick was in school, overall attitudes toward the disabled have improved dramatically.

I knew Aaron and Michelle were proud of Nick, yet they weren't all that happy to be constantly referred to as Nick's brother or Nick's sister, which is understandable. What I did not know until recently was that Michelle went through a period when she feared being ostracized because of her oldest brother. She was entering those socially tumultuous teen years when this occurred.

At the time Michelle was afraid other girls would shun her or think she was strange because she had a brother without limbs. She also worried that boys wouldn't want to date her because of Nick. Social workers say this is very typical for siblings at that age. Most young people in their teen years suffer from rampant insecurities and an overpowering need to fit in and be accepted. Michelle may have had her fears, but she kept her concerns about being Nick's sister to herself. I don't recall any major blowups or breakdowns. She was a pretty popular kid with many friends, male and female.

A few years later in an interview, she was quite open about Nick's positive impact on her life. "Being his sister made me realize that kids with a disability are no different from anyone else. I don't even see their disability. I just go straight to their heart and soul. It is there that I find pure love and joy and, most of all, a human being."

THE UPSIDE FOR SIBLINGS

While there are some common challenges in growing up with a special-needs sibling, there are benefits to be derived as well. The literature on this usually cites potential sibling benefits such as a more mature outlook than age-group peers; more empathy and a greater willingness to help others less fortunate; stronger coping and problem-solving skills; greater gratitude for things most people take for granted; more patience; enhanced teamwork skills; and a more open heart toward those with disabilities, chronic illness, and special needs.

I'd have to say that both Aaron and Michelle have experienced most of those benefits after growing up with Nick. Those of us who have lived with him through the good times and bad have been affected in many positive ways.

There is some debate among sociologists who study the impact of a disabled child on siblings when it comes to their career choices. For a long time, I'd heard it said that a higher than normal percentage of people with disabled siblings went into careers in health care, teaching special education, and social work. Recently I've read that has been called into question, but our family has one example.

Michelle obtained her nursing degree and, after working as an emergency room nurse for three years, she served on several missions to give medical care to people without easy access to it. One of her most remarkable experiences came at the age of twenty-three when she volunteered to spend three months as a nurse aboard the world's largest private hospital ship, the

Africa Mercy, anchored off the West African nation of Togo. She had learned about the floating hospital from Nick, who had visited it while on a speaking tour in Africa.

You have to be committed to volunteer to serve in the *Mercy's* hospital because they require that you pay your own room and board during your stay. Michelle sold her car and used her savings to pay her way because she was longing to do work that helped her grow and made a difference in the world for people in need.

Dushka's career as a nurse and midwife certainly had some influence on Michelle's pursuit of a nursing degree too. Our daughter has a giving nature, and she sometimes gives too much, so I was glad when she took a break to earn a degree in music production, which is her other passion—one she shares with Nick.

Now that all three of our children are adults, I think it's safe to say that our efforts to nurture them all equally and to make sure they all felt loved and supported were successful. There is no resentment from Aaron and Michelle toward their brother for all the attention he received. I know this because in 2015 both Michelle and Aaron moved to California to work with their brother and to support him in his Life Without Limbs nonprofit and his Attitude Is Altitude business. One of the greatest rewards of our lives is having all our children together, watching them talk and laugh, celebrate each other's successes, and support each other as adults.

TAKEAWAY THOUGHTS

- Your child's siblings can be best friends and allies or resentful rivals for your affections and attention, so it is very important to take every opportunity early on to give them as much of your love and time as possible so they don't feel left out.

- Siblings may feel resentment if the disabled child is not disciplined or assigned chores or is otherwise given a pass on things for which the siblings are held accountable. So whenever possible, it is best to allow the disabled child no special treatment.

- It's important to educate your other children about the causes, nature, and impact of their sibling's disabilities. They need to fully understand that they are not at risk of "catching" the disability and that the disabled child may not be able to do all they can do but that he or she still needs and desires their love and support. Teenage siblings can have complex and contradictory feelings about a disabled brother or sister during those years when being accepted and fitting in socially becomes so important. Be aware of this and do your best to help keep their family bonds strong.

- Try not to saddle siblings with responsibilities for the disabled child. It puts too much pressure on them and may stir up resentment.

- Talk to the siblings about what they can learn from having a special-needs brother or sister and what they can tell their friends about him or her.

Nick trying out his
baby prosthetic arms

An early outing with Dad at the beach

The Vujicic family
in the early days

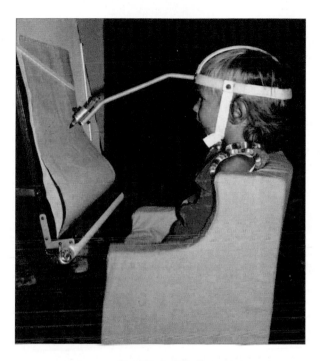

"I can do this."

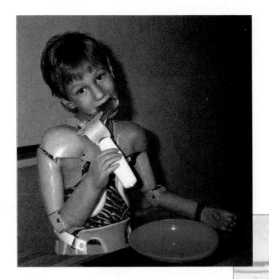

Always determined to live
a life without limits

More sporting adventures

Our family today, left to right: Kanae, Kiyoshi, Nick, Boris, Dejan, Dushka, daughter Michelle, daughter-in-law Michelle, Aaron

Nick inspiring young people

Proud father and son

Nick's platform stretches
around the globe.

Seven

Nick in the Mainstream

Champion Your Child's Education

When we first attempted to enroll Nick in private school, we must have missed a sign on the door of the principal's office:

No Arms.

No Legs.

No Admittance.

And that was a private Christian school!

We had already experienced some discriminatory behavior and even shunning of our son and were recommended to Yooralla, a special school for the disabled. However, we were determined to mainstream Nick and got him accepted and enrolled in Albanvale Kindergarten. The goal of kindergarten was to prepare him for entering elementary school, when he would be moving outside the protective cocoon of our family.

There was a risk in that, certainly, and we quickly discovered there were individuals and institutions that did not open their arms to our disabled son. The other kids in the kindergarten generally were fine with Nick because they hadn't formed prejudices against the disabled. Unfortunately, some of their mothers were not so open minded. Dushka tried to convince them that having Nick in the group would not cause the arms and legs of all the other children to fall off.

Nick's kindergarten experience was good. It was a half-day program, and the teacher was quite accepting and accommodating. Things changed dramatically, however, when it came time to enroll Nick in primary school. Most parents simply go to a neighborhood private or public school and enroll their children with no questions asked. Whenever we tried to enroll Nick, we hit a wall as soon as we mentioned that he had a physical disability.

Since we are Christians and very focused on the church community, our first inclination was to enroll Nick in a private Christian school. We felt he would get more personal attention in a smaller school. Most were more expensive than public schools, but thanks to Nick's aunts and uncles, we had the funds to pay for his tuition and expenses. They had created an education fund for him shortly after birth.

We made the mistake of thinking that private Christian schools would be more tolerant and accepting—Dushka and I were lifelong Christians, after all. Yet once we explained to administrators that Nick was not the typical student, they declined to accept him as a student. Nick's disabilities were a major concern for the principals, teaching staff, students, and parents we met with. They regarded Nick as an unwanted burden who would tax their limited resources. These are some of the objections we encountered:

- We don't have wheelchair-accessible classrooms.
- We don't have funding for the teachers' assistants he would require.
- How would he write? Draw? Cut with scissors?
- What about his personal hygiene?
- We don't have wheelchair-accessible bathrooms or anyone who could help him use them.
- How would he feed himself in the cafeteria?
- How could we guarantee his safety on the playground?
- We're afraid he'd make the other kids uncomfortable.

It was probably just as well. Nick was growing up in a Christian family, and most of our friends were Christian, so putting him in a Christian school might have limited his range of experience and his social connections. We certainly didn't want him to grow up isolated from the rest of the world.

JOINING THE MAINSTREAM

The most common recommendation given to us by the Christian school administrators was to have Nick attend a public segregated school for disabled students. In the past, the government had supported a segregated educational environment to provide an education while meeting the unique needs of these children. These schools received special funding from the government to educate special-needs children. They were all wheelchair and handicap accessible. The teachers were specially trained for special-needs kids. This was an easy option for them to suggest, but we could not accept it.

We did not want Nick to be placed in a school that was strictly for disabled kids. On paper it made sense. In reality it just didn't work for us. We felt that environment would not be in Nick's best interests over the long term. After our visit to the Yooralla school for the disabled, we had decided we did not want Nick to attend that type of school because of the segregated environment. Nick had taught us from an early age that his disabilities did not define him. He refused to accept limits on his life, and we weren't about to stifle his independent and positive spirit. Sooner or later, Nick would have to live and work among the general population. Our feeling was the more he learned to deal with the real world, the better. Children are much more adaptable than adults. We thought Nick would find a way to fit in.

Because Nick had already experienced some rejection, we realized that in a public school he might well have to deal with prejudice, taunting, and bullying. We had great concerns about that, of course, but every child deals with those things to some degree. At some point, you have to let them venture from the nest and figure out how to exist in the world.

We knew we had to be strong. Parents can't protect their children from every possible hurt, as much as we might like to. Well-meaning social workers and educators told us Nick would fit best in the schools designed for special-needs kids. We decided to reject their advice and go with our instincts—and Nick's yearning for a normal life. He wanted to be accepted as a regular kid.

Over the years we consulted experts and listened to their advice, but Nick is so unique that often the standard rules and approaches did not apply. No two children are alike. Doctors, social workers, and psychologists tend to pin labels on them and then apply treatments accordingly. They didn't take into account Nick's determination and his ability to rise above the expectations of others. We wanted to give him the opportunity to thrive in the mainstream, so we began searching for a suitable public school in our area.

PARENT ACTIVISTS

After decades of segregating special-needs students, Australia was just beginning to open its mainstream schools to the disabled. Public schools were cleared to accept them, but many were not yet equipped with ramps, handicap restrooms, and other necessary features. Dushka and I became activists on Nick's behalf, lobbying the Department of Education to provide funds for teachers' aides and to allow volunteers in the classroom for special-needs kids.

Through the efforts of many people, the doors of public schools were opened. Nick became a member of the first class of special-needs students allowed to attend regular public schools in our district. The next challenge was finding a school able to accommodate him.

We checked out several established elementary schools, but once again, we found their administrators and staff were not encouraging. Despite the national mainstreaming movement, they claimed they were not yet equipped to handle a wheelchair student with no limbs.

Finally one of our relatives recommended a newly constructed primary school in a new residential development in northwest Melbourne. The school was Keilor Downs, and it had been built to meet the needs of mainstreamed disabled and special-needs students. Classrooms were on one level with ramp access for wheelchairs, wide hallways, and accessible restrooms.

This was an exciting discovery for us on several fronts. The school was the first we'd found that was so well suited for Nick and his wheelchair, and the surrounding Keilor Downs neighborhood had lots for new-home construction that were within our price range. Our home at the time was an older place that wasn't suited for Nick's wheelchair anyway because it had stairs and narrow hallways.

We decided if Keilor Downs Elementary School accepted Nick, we would build a new house custom designed for his needs and within walking distance of the school. We also liked the fact that this was a brand-new school for all the students, so everyone would be "the new kid" and, hopefully, it would be easier for Nick to make friends and find acceptance.

TEAM NICK

The timing was good because the educational environment was changing. That school year the Victoria state school system allowed thirty-five hundred disabled children to join mainstream classes in one thousand schools. Nick was part of this first wave, which required many adjustments by administrators, teachers, and other parents.

We met with the principal at Keilor Downs, who expressed his support and willingness to admit Nick as a student. He noted that there would be some preparation necessary before he could make it happen. He had to get his teaching staff trained so they could adjust their methods and materials. They would also have to work with the other students and their parents to make sure Nick was welcomed and accepted.

In today's more open-minded environment, it's hard to believe some parents expressed concerns that Nick would be a distraction or that he would require so much extra attention that it might take away from the time teachers devoted to their children. Yet there were those who offered those arguments. Fortunately they were in the minority.

There was also government bureaucracy and the inevitable financial considerations to deal with. The local and state education department had to provide adequate funding for a teacher's aide to assist Nick, as well as a special desk with enough clearance for his wheelchair. The education department conducted an assessment of Nick and his needs, which included a doctor's evaluation to determine his ability to function in the classroom alongside other students. The school formed a sort of Team Nick committee to pave the way for him. It was comprised of the principal, Nick's teachers, the teacher's aide, Dushka, a physician, and a representative from the education department.

We were grateful then and remain thankful today for the Keilor Downs principal and his willingness to take on this challenge. He was a Baptist, by the way. I don't know if being a Christian influenced his decision. I tend to think he simply had a good heart. Perhaps it was both. Whatever his motivation, we thank God for this man and his decision because even though there were obstacles to overcome, our son thrived in the mainstream environment.

Dushka played a big role as Nick's chief advocate during his early school years. To handle those duties, she went on a part-time schedule for her nursing job. This cut into our income, but we felt it was best for her to take an active role in Nick's education. My dad also helped out by coming to our house during the school year to pick up Nick and then drop him off at school whenever we needed his assistance. My mother did her part too, looking after all our kids whenever Dushka and I were working.

GOOD TIMING

As I noted earlier, technological advancements have played such a big role in Nick's life that I've sometimes wondered if God has a branch office in Silicon Valley. This was especially true in his school. The introduction of desktop computers in the classroom was a great benefit. Nick could not hold a book, but he could read a computer screen, and he could type on a keyboard and manipulate a mouse or a joystick with his left foot.

We worked with his teachers to help Nick in the classroom in other ways. Dushka and I used Aquaplast—a moldable plastic material often used in hospitals to create splints—to create a holder for his pens and pencils that fit onto his left foot. He could use it to write and draw with greater ease.

I built a desktop stand that stored his writing materials in a manner that gave Nick easy access to them. It was quite a strain on him to write for lengthy periods, so his teachers' aides took notes in class for Nick. Still, he was able to use his foot to do many tasks. We even improvised a way for him to use scissors. We embedded one side of the scissors handle into the desktop storage container. He could insert papers and press down on the other handle of the scissors to make a cut.

We knew that integrating Nick into the classroom would have its challenges, but the rewards were worth it. Even the simplest classroom activities test the ingenuity and patience of a student with no limbs. Yet with the help and understanding of those around him, Nick persevered.

OUR POSTER CHILD

From the first grade onward, we kept Nick in the mainstream. It wasn't exactly a sink-or-swim situation because we were always there to support him, but Nick did have to fight to stay afloat sometimes. Fear of rejection by classmates and sometimes impatience from teachers could have caused irreparable damage to our child, yet Nick's success and achievements in school astounded not only Dushka and me but also his principal, teachers, social workers, and other family members. Even the parents of the other students, whom we feared would see Nick as an unwelcome and even intimidating distraction, came to embrace and celebrate our son.

Again, the credit goes to Nick. He did not hide in a corner of the lunchroom. He reached out to the other kids. He spoke up in class. He made jokes, often at his own expense. He engaged with everyone around him. The same charismatic qualities that would one day lead to his becoming one of the world's most popular public speakers were emerging, though we weren't aware at the time.

In the years since Nick first entered the mainstream school population, many parents of disabled kids have told us that our son served as a role model for their kids. Because Nick overcame doubts and won the affection of his classmates and teachers, it became easier and more acceptable for other kids with challenges to follow him. Their parents saw that Nick was accepted and accommodated, so they were more open to allowing their special-needs children to enter the mainstream.

It is no exaggeration to say that Nick became a symbol for the integration of children with disabilities into the education system in Australia. Officials from the Department of Education and state politicians visited Nick's school to talk with him and his teachers and to observe him interacting with his classmates. Television and newspaper reporters and photographers interviewed him.

This was his first exposure to the media spotlight, and as you might expect, Nick welcomed it like a flower soaks up sunshine. His positive and inspiring attitude blossomed. Dushka and I were delighted that the rest of the world had the opportunity to meet the real Nick. It was quite telling, also, that when Nick spoke to the media, he naturally assumed the role of spokesman and role model for all disabled and special-needs kids.

The government was pouring money into the campaign to mainstream special-needs students. Officials were looking for kids to serve as examples and to speak in support of integration. Nick's passion and positive messages in the media drew the attention of the Australian Department of Education. The education minister, Joan Kirner, became quite a fan of Nick, which proved to be very helpful. She visited Nick's school in 1988 and had her photograph taken with Nick for a newspaper article headlined "Trailblazer Nicholas." Shortly thereafter, the funding to help Victorian schools mainstream Nick and other special-needs students was increased to 3.7 million dollars. Part of that funding was to integrate two more disabled students the next year to follow Nick's trail. Joan Kirner later became the first woman to hold the position of premier of our state.

In 1991, Nick was named Keilor's Junior Citizen of the Year for "courage beyond his years" and was also nominated for Young Australian of the Year in 2001. There were other awards, acknowledgments, and recognitions over his school years.

We were grateful that Nick was thought of as a good example for the integration program in Australia's schools. He handled the attention well. Nevertheless, we had to exercise caution and ensure he kept his ego in check and didn't become cocky. We became more protective of our privacy and put limits on Nick's time in the spotlight. There was also a concern about our other kids being in his shadow. It was a unique problem to have—a disabled child becoming a media sensation—so we had to be creative in handling it.

SEEDS PLANTED

None of us had any idea at the time certainly, but these experiences likely planted the seeds for Nick's public-speaking career. He became very comfortable talking to the media and large groups while offering his views on the value of mainstream education for disabled kids. Later, in the early days of his speaking career, the MacGregor State School principal became a big supporter. He predicted our son would be a great achiever and that one day he would be paid more than ten thousand dollars to speak in public. We took it as a compliment, of course, but found it a little hard to believe at the time. Today Nick's corporate speaking fees often are considerably more than that amount, so the principal should be credited with his foresight.

Our early decision to actively socialize our son by mainstreaming him and encouraging him to reach out and speak up was already having quite a positive impact, not only on his life but also on the lives of other disabled kids. Nick attended Keilor Downs through the first part of fourth grade, and then we moved from Melbourne to Brisbane, Queensland.

NEW KID IN CLASS

When we left the comfortable life we'd created in Melbourne, Dushka and I worried it would be hard on Nick to leave so many friends and family members behind. One of his teachers warned that his new school might not be as welcoming for Nick, saying, "You don't know how good you have had it here."

At first we worried that might be true when we struggled to get Nick accepted in another school. After several failed attempts, we had success at Gold Coast Robina Primary School. Nick felt at home there because his teacher had a disability that required her to be in a wheelchair too. He was there for just one semester, however. He then was transferred to MacGregor State School in Brisbane, which was a much larger school than either Robina or Keilor Downs. The school district moved him because it wanted disabled students in the more modern school designed to accommodate them and their needs.

We had fears initially, but MacGregor proved to be an even better place for our son. This school had a well-established mainstreaming program and other children in wheelchairs too, so Dushka and I didn't have to be quite so involved in creating a good environment for Nick. Teachers had more experience with adjusting their lesson plans for disabled and special-needs kids. It helped that Nick was no longer the only student in a wheelchair, which made things much easier for him and for us.

Nick has always had a knack for overcoming his loneliness and insecurities by becoming part of a cause greater than himself. Somehow he instinctively figured out that helping others was the best strategy for helping himself. At MacGregor he joined fundraising drives and charitable projects. For one of the fundraisers, Nick and his classmates competed in selling goods door to door, and he became the top salesman in the school.

Joining in on school projects allowed him to get to know the other students and teachers. They learned quickly that while Nick lacked arms and legs, he possessed a keen mind, a terrific sense of humor, and a smile that drew people to him. He managed to win over so many of his fellow students that Nick was elected MacGregor's school captain in 1995, which is equivalent to being named president of the entire student body.

In that role, Nick led the student council in its effort to raise five thousand dollars for a fitness center at MacGregor, where his name is still displayed on a plaque honoring all former school captains. We found it quite humorous that one of Nick's campaign platforms was to conduct wheelchair races as a regular school activity. I don't think he ever delivered on that promise, by the way.

Nick was the first disabled student to lead his classmates at MacGregor. He later achieved a similar honor in high school. That was particularly impressive because that school, Runcorn High School, was in a different school district than his primary school. We had to send him to Runcorn because the usual high school for MacGregor kids was not wheelchair accessible. As a result, Nick had to start all over, prove himself, and make new friends.

STARTING OVER

When Nick entered Runcorn, he was once again placed in the role of new kid. All his primary school friends went to another high school. Nick had three things working against him in his new environment: he was the unknown kid, he had an unusual body, and he was in a wheelchair.

Public acceptance of disabled students has come a long way since Nick's high school years. He has played a big role in changing those perceptions by speaking at schools around the world and posting inspiring videos popular with young people. Unfortunately, back in his high school days, it wasn't considered cool to hang out with "the wheelchair kid." His new classmates saw Nick's limbless body and the big bulky wheelchair and they made all sorts of negative assumptions about him. Poor Nick had already gone through this process of proving himself and making friends repeatedly. We couldn't blame him for feeling discouraged at first.

Nick has written and talked about his struggles to fit in during his early high school years. Until recently, Dushka and I hadn't known that he'd gone so far as to take up cursing because he thought it would help him win acceptance with a group of "cool kids." Nick isn't proud of that decision, and I was glad to hear that he was quite terrible at cursing and gave it up out of embarrassment.

CAPTAIN COURAGEOUS

Nick admits he strayed from his Christian upbringing for a brief time. He declined invitations to join prayer sessions and hang out with the Christian kids because he didn't want to be put in a box by other classmates. It's not unusual for teenagers to question their family's faith. We understood that, even if we didn't like it. Nick still hadn't come to terms with why God had denied him arms and legs.

He struggled, and while it was hard to watch, it revealed a lot about our son's strength of character. We weren't even aware of the cursing and the rejection of his Christian classmates, so we weren't on his case about these bad decisions. The impressive thing is that Nick eventually realized he'd made those mistakes, and he self-corrected. The ability to do that is critical to success in life. Once we become adults, the quality of our decisions has a major impact on the quality of our lives. Our parents aren't there to steer us and show us the way. We have to figure things out for ourselves. We all make mistakes, so it is critical that we also become capable of admitting them and changing our behavior to get better results.

Nick checked his actions against the root values he'd grown up with, and he put himself back in line with those values. This was a major step toward growing the wings necessary to fly on his own as a young man. Once Nick quit trying to be what he thought others wanted him to be, his classmates were drawn to him. He made friends and became a leader in his school.

As I noted earlier, his success in the mainstream of the education system throughout his school years brought Nick a lot of media attention. One of my favorite headlines from his school days hailed him as "Captain Courageous." We liked that. Dushka and I were always impressed that Nick did so well when interviewed by the media. He didn't dwell on his own achievements, but instead he humbly encouraged other special-needs kids to stand strong and share their talents and gifts. Perhaps my favorite newspaper quote from Nick during his school years was this simple, uplifting response he gave to a reporter who asked what his election to school captain meant to other kids with disabilities.

"All wheelchair kids, I reckon, should just give everything a go!" he said.

His message was "We have value. We are just like everyone else. Don't segregate us. Don't label us. Don't put limits on us. Allow us to show you what we can do despite the challenges of our disabilities." Through his example, Nick taught us all a great deal about the power of removing labels and limits on the disabled and giving them the freedom to flourish.

TARGETED BY BULLIES

With the freedom of being in the mainstream comes exposure to both the good and the bad, of course. Because he changed schools several times as we moved around, he spent more time than most as "the new kid." This role is never easy, and you can only imagine how difficult it was to be the new kid who has no arms and no legs.

When we moved from Melbourne to Brisbane, to the United States, and then back to Brisbane, we did so to try to make life better for Nick. Unfortunately it didn't always work out that way. When we first moved to Brisbane, he went through a long period of isolation. He was hesitant to speak up or to reach out and try to make friends. He withdrew and tended to stay to himself at first. He often talks about how he hid in the bushes on the playground or in a corner of the classroom.

Nick had been a star student at Keilor Downs; it was difficult for him to be ignored or anonymous. He was hesitant to speak up or to extend himself to make friends. This was the period when Nick began to obsess over his future and his purpose. He went through a period of despair. He was afraid he'd always be a burden on us. These dark thoughts drove him to attempt suicide.

He has written in his own books that a contributing factor to his suicidal thoughts was bullying from schoolmates. His most infamous bullying encounter occurred in the first grade at Keilor Downs, and it culminated in a dramatic playground fight. Neither Dushka nor I were present so we can only take Nick's word for it, but he claims to have vanquished his much larger opponent by head-butting him in the nose.

This fight, which has taken on mythological status among our son's fans, led to the creation of a favorite Nick motto: "Armless, but not harmless." While he is a major advocate of nonviolence, Nick maintains that the first-grade bully gave him no choice but to defend himself. He kept goading Nick and threatening to beat him up. It was Nick's first and last fight. We are very grateful that he retired from the ring undefeated.

Nick's account of that fight is actually quite funny to read or hear about, but I don't want to make light of bullying or its impact on Nick and other victims. There were several instances in grade school and high school when Nick felt so intimidated and fearful that he did not want to leave the house.

Bullies are often the victims of bullying themselves. They inflict suffering on others because older siblings, other kids, or cruel parents have tormented them. Some bullies, though, are just mean spirited. It's also true that a few are misguided. They mistakenly believe their taunts and shoves are little more than teasing or kidding around.

Just as there are different types of bullies, there are a number of ways for dealing with them. We never advised Nick to try to fight bullies who wanted to hurt him physically. Instead, we told him to report them to his teachers and school administrators while staying out of their reach.

STANDING STRONG

Nick faced bullies who intimidated him for long periods, but in most cases, he stood up for himself in some fashion. I wouldn't recommend that parents advise their children to fight or confront bullies. Instead, the best tactic is to seek the support of school administrators and the protection of teachers and friends.

Still, Nick did manage to rid himself of one bully who made his life miserable for a while in high school. He was mortified when this classmate began yelling out the same nasty taunt every time he saw our son in the hallways or on campus. Nick tried to avoid his tormentor as much as possible, which was wise. When the harassment went on for several weeks, Nick finally confronted his bully. He told him that his words were hurtful and asked him to stop. I think Nick was surprised when the bully seemed contrite and said he'd really meant no harm. The other guy claimed he was just kidding him, and he promptly stopped after Nick asked him to end the taunting.

Even when that bullying episode ended, it bothered Nick that no other students had stood up for him. Few kids escape bullying altogether while growing up. Studies have found that kids with disabilities and special needs are targeted more than others. Bullies tend to focus on an individual's weaknesses or anything that makes them different or especially vulnerable.

Dushka and I tried to be supportive and put things in perspective for Nick. We urged him to filter out cruel comments, whether they were intentional or not. We told him not to take taunts or shunning to heart. The best revenge in those cases, we said, is to have fun with people who do enjoy his company.

The fact is that parents can only do so much to protect and insulate their children from bullying and cruelty during their school years. We also felt that to some degree, it was good for Nick to understand that in the real world, not everyone would love and accept him. A hard heart is not a good thing, but a tough skin can be a real asset. We never allowed Nick to hide from bullies by skipping school. As a result, he developed a courageous spirit.

Thanks to the efforts of antibullying campaigns and advocates like Nick, awareness has increased in recent years. School administrators, parents, and kids realize that bullying is a serious issue. This movement to stop bullying was inspired by growing concern that kids around the world were being terrorized and even pushed to suicide by verbal, physical, and online bullying.

CAMPAIGNING AGAINST CRUELTY

Bullying affects nearly every family to some degree, but it is particularly heartbreaking for those with disabled and special-needs kids because our children already have substantial burdens. Cruelty from their peers can threaten to destroy all the efforts parents put into building self-esteem and strong character in their kids.

It is heartening to see more and more schools bring this issue to the forefront with active antibullying programs. Our hearts soar when we see students reach out to their disabled classmates, protect them, and make them feel welcome and valued. One of the great things about mainstreaming our children is that other students learn that special-needs kids are individuals too. They get to know the unique people who are more than their disabilities and challenges. They see that they have strong personalities along with talents and gifts to give the world.

Nick and other antibullying activists encourage young people to embrace their disabled classmates rather than isolate them. We can learn from each other, certainly. In his antibullying book, *Stand Strong*, Nick offers many lessons that kids can use to protect themselves against bullying. I won't repeat them here. I do advise parents of special-needs school-age kids that their best offense can be a good defense. The best way you can prepare your child to handle bullying effectively is to help him build a strong sense of his own value in this world. Let him know he is loved and worthy of love. Help him identify his talents and gifts and guide him in building upon them so he sees that he has a purpose in this world.

When you discipline your special-needs child, try to do it without criticizing her or belittling her because that only takes away from her self-esteem and makes her more vulnerable to the cruelty of bullies. Most of all, keep your lines of communication open and spend time observing your child among her classmates so that if bullying is occurring, you can pick up on it and stop it before it escalates.

Kids with mental disabilities sometimes don't understand that they are being bullied. They may not have the ability to discern when a bully is pretending to be their friend but is actually taking advantage of them or ridiculing them. That is another reason it is so important for parents to stay engaged and monitor their children's relationships closely. We tried to avoid becoming helicopter parents hovering over Nick, but we made an effort to talk regularly with his teachers and many of his classmates on a regular basis.

If children have difficulty communicating emotions, you can ask them to make drawings of happy or sad faces or to use their favorite possession to act out their school days and their interactions with other students. Encourage them to keep a journal that you can read with them, or ask them to give you a top-ten list of how their school week went.

I've seen other special-needs kids respond with great enthusiasm to my son's antibullying videos, which you can find on YouTube or on the websites for his *Stand Strong* book and for his organizations, Life Without Limbs and

Attitude Is Altitude. Nick has been there, and he has great advice and encouragement to offer kids who are dealing with bullies.

Nick encourages special-needs and disabled students to be comfortable with themselves and to dare to reach out to other kids. He also advocates that they be proactive. He tells young people who are feeling down to counter their despair by reaching out and helping others. His positive message empowers them to be the miracle they seek, to help someone else find the healing they want for themselves. You can't ever go wrong following that advice.

PROTECTING EACH OTHER

Some kids are bullied because they are short, have pimples, or lack athletic ability. Imagine what it must have been like for Nick as a teen who was so very different from all his classmates. He was in his midtwenties before he met another person born with no arms and no legs. He was often the only student in a wheelchair in his school. He wrote and typed and drew with a little foot that was unlike anything his classmates had ever seen. Nick was different in ways that could not be hidden from sight. He couldn't just blend in.

When they first met Nick, it was natural for his classmates to stare at him, be wary of him, and ask questions that sometimes embarrassed him. He is so unusual in appearance that we told him he should expect the other kids to act that way. Our advice was for him to show them he was just a normal kid who skateboarded, played video games, and loved movies.

"Talk to them. Joke with them. Show them that you are just like them in every other way," we said.

It took courage for Nick to do that. Some days he didn't want to leave the house. We felt his pain, but we told him that he could not hide from the world. Dushka and I assured him that he could win acceptance if he showed strength and believed in himself.

"If you want people to be a friend to you, then be a friend to them," we said. "You can't expect kindness and understanding if you don't give it. You reap what you sow."

Nick had some rough patches, but in general, he thrived as a mainstream student. He had bad days, even bad weeks and months, yet he learned to persevere and to prove himself. Dushka and I were proud of him because Nick didn't just stand strong; he stood out and became a leader in his school years.

One of our favorite memories of those times occurred during his first year in primary school. Dushka and I were deeply moved when we visited the school and observed Nick's first-grade classmates joking with him, carrying his school bags, and working with him on projects. We were also a bit surprised when Nick came home a few days later and announced that he'd won a marbles match on the playground.

"How do you play marbles?" Dushka asked.

"I roll my marble with my foot, and if I hit someone else's marble, I get to keep it," he said.

Then he held up a large bag fairly bursting with his hard-won marbles.

That's our son. He always goes for *all* the marbles!

TAKEAWAY THOUGHTS

- As with medical matters, we recommend that parents see themselves as active advocates for the education of their disabled children. You cannot assume that any principal, teacher, teacher's aide, classmate, or classmate's parent cares as much about your child or knows your child as well as you do.
- We found that the best approach was to enlist school administrators, teachers, and teachers' aides in a Team Nick program

that included regular communication, coordination of schedules, and a clear understanding of our child's needs, expectations, strengths, weaknesses, and goals.

- We tried never to openly criticize or be combative with teachers even if we disagreed with them, because we did not want them to treat Nick poorly or resent him.
- We were quite involved in school activities and programs to show that we were engaged in our child's education.
- It can be daunting these days, but we recommend that parents understand the laws and regulations regarding the rights of disabled children and the requirements for educating them in their school system.
- Keep detailed records of your child's grades, assessment tests, and communications with school administrators and teachers.
- Make an effort to be aware of government funding, charitable organizations, and special programs that can benefit the disabled in your school system. Your child may be eligible for more help than you might think.
- Closely monitor your child's moods and attitude toward school so you can detect if bullying is an issue. Talk to your child regularly about how he or she gets along with classmates and consult with the teacher and school administrators if you suspect there is a problem.

Eight

Roots and Wings

Prepare Your Child
for Adulthood

The "take it day by day" parenting approach we adapted early on with Nick was a defensive move on our part. We had to raise Nick. We couldn't spend our days fretting about his future. Neither of us could imagine back then how a person without limbs might support himself in adulthood. That approach had to change once Nick entered his teen years. With adulthood approaching, we shifted our focus to helping our son find a career path.

We felt a responsibility to give Nick and all our children roots and wings. The term *roots* refers to providing a child with a solid foundation that typically includes knowing that he is loved and valued along with basic life skills, a sense of personal responsibility, a strong value system, and a spiritual base.

The term *wings* refers to what happens after you provide that foundation and a child reaches adulthood. It is then time to step back and give the child room to grow, to make mistakes and learn from them, and eventually, to become independent and self-sufficient. If your children are capable and competent, the goal with roots and wings is to one day see them leave the nest and fly on their own as self-supporting and successful adults.

Parents with disabled and special-needs kids often say that next to the initial diagnosis period, the greatest challenges come when their children are done with school and enter adulthood. Many special-needs kids can never attain complete independence because of substantial physical and mental challenges. Their parents and families often face difficult decisions, though there seem to be greater opportunities today for many to live independently with assistance from caregivers or special housing, community living, and group homes.

Our initial concerns that Nick might never be able to support himself were dispelled when he proved to be a good student with an entrepreneurial drive. We thought he would always need a caregiver to assist him, but he also proved to be remarkably independent in many ways.

Parents want the best for their children, and we tend to be more conservative in our vision for their futures. I thought Nick's lack of limbs would restrict him to some sort of office job. He had more ambitious dreams, as it turned out.

When Nick entered his high school years, we still had no solid grasp of how our son would live independently. We prayed for guidance, and in the meantime, we did our best to make sure he studied and took classes that gave him a good basic education to build upon. Our goal was simply to help him attain self-sufficiency by finding a career path that he could follow to whatever heights he wanted to achieve. This is the goal of most parents for their children. We weren't about to force him into doing something that did not interest him, so we talked with him about his interests and what career choices appealed to him. He was quite good at math and working with computers, which opened up many possibilities.

Music was another strong interest for our son, who still sings and plays an electronic drum kit. He participated in a percussion band, playing drums and the xylophone in high school and in church. His high school jazz-band teacher, who was fond of Nick, allowed him to conduct the band during some performances. Nick even received a jazz merit award in high school, and he sometimes talked about pursuing a career in music.

Gentle Guidance

As his pragmatic father, I worried that the options for a well-paying, stable career were pretty limited in the music business, especially for someone who lacked limbs. I was trained as a business accountant, so I worked with him to build on his inherent talent for mathematics. We made learning multiplication tables a fun thing for him and Aaron. They competed to see who could correctly answer math problems first.

I encouraged Nick in this area because some of the greatest job opportunities seemed to involve math and computer skills. Desktop computers and laptops were quickly becoming standard in many industries, and Nick, who was an avid video-game player, was adept at working with a computer keyboard, mouse, and joystick with his foot. In his final year of high school, he did an internship with the IT help desk at Queen Elizabeth II Jubilee Hospital in Sunnybank, Brisbane. Nick answered calls and logged the jobs. He was paid well and received positive feedback, but he wasn't thrilled about working at a desk all day.

A Greater Vision

There is a saying that man makes plans and God laughs. The Almighty One must be highly amused at my plans to prepare Nick for a job as a numbers cruncher. There are no sure-fire or guaranteed plans for helping a disabled child attain self-sufficiency. Ultimately they have to make their own choices if they are capable adults. It takes incredible drive and determination for those with special challenges to succeed and thrive. All we can do as parents is support them and help them do the best they can.

My son sometimes felt I was pushing him into tougher classes than he wanted to take. My dad, who was close to Nick and often picked him up from school, even stepped in to say he thought I was expecting too much of Nick. My father argued that I shouldn't have the same expectations for Nick that fathers had for their "normal children" when it came to getting a job and supporting himself one day.

I told my dad that we had watched Nick accomplish things we had never dreamed possible. In fact, Dushka and I developed something of an immunity to being shocked by Nick's overachieving ways. We'd reached the point where his feats would just leave us shrugging and saying, "Yep, that's Nick! There's no stopping him."

As it turned out, Nick found his wings and a career path that he loved with a little help from an unlikely source—his high school janitor.

A HELPING HEART

When Nick transferred to Runcorn High School, he could no longer ride the bus home after school because we lived in a different district. As a result, he usually had to wait for us to come get him, and our work schedules often made us late.

Nick usually had to hang out at school for an hour before we could come pick him up. He had managed to make a few friends by this time, but if they weren't around, Nick would find himself talking to Mr. Arnold, the high school's janitor. That job title does not capture either the spiritual nature or the contributions of this man who served as a mentor for our son and many of his classmates. Nick described Mr. Arnold as a person so at peace and filled with faith that "he glowed from within."

Mr. Arnold was also an observant and wise man. In the opening weeks of the school year, he noticed that Nick hadn't made many friends and appeared withdrawn and sad. He reached out to Nick and befriended him. They often talked in the school lobby while Nick waited for his ride home.

One day Mr. Arnold invited Nick to join a Christian youth group that he led during the lunch hour at school. Nick had not spent much time with the school's Christian kids, but he liked Mr. Arnold so he agreed to go. For the first several meetings, Nick didn't participate much, but Mr. Arnold kept encouraging him to talk about himself and his faith. "We want to know more about you, Nick," he said.

Finally Nick agreed to speak up at the next meeting. He'd been lonely and isolated. He saw this as an opportunity to let the other kids know that the guy in the wheelchair was no different from them. He was so nervous that he prepared note cards with talking points.

Nick spoke from the heart at the meeting, sharing stories about what it was like to be a new kid in school who was so different physically but still had the same desire to be accepted and appreciated. Nick told them that some fellow students had shunned him because they assumed he was mentally handicapped on top of his physical disabilities. He confessed that he'd sometimes wondered how a loving God could create him without limbs. He'd questioned whether there was any purpose for his life. "I'm trying to have faith that I wasn't just a mistake," he said.

His audience was moved by his story and inspired by his humanity, faith, and courage. I've often thought that Nick's career as a public speaker began on that day. After his talk, Nick felt as though he'd released a burden he'd carried for a long time. He nearly broke down crying. He was surprised to see that the students in the group were emotional too. Many of them had tears in their eyes at the end of his talk.

"Was I that bad?" he asked Mr. Arnold.

"No, Nick, you were that good!"

Nick thought his friend was just being nice, but then one of the students in the group invited Nick to speak to his church's youth organization. Another one asked if he'd talk to his Sunday school class. Soon he was fielding requests to speak to church groups, youth organizations, and student clubs.

Dushka and I weren't all that aware of Nick's early speaking engagements because he kept them to himself, but we did notice some changes. His attitude about school became more positive. He also began to show a much greater interest in going to church. Within a few months, Nick announced that he wanted to be a Christian and he committed his life to his faith.

God's Stealthy Ways

I don't want to say that God is sneaky, but He can be very subtle, like a chess master who is always six moves ahead of his opponent. I make that observation because around this same time in his school career, Nick heard his first live presentation by a motivational and inspirational speaker by the name of Reggie Dabbs, an American who speaks to young people all over the world.

Reggie managed to captivate nearly fourteen hundred hot and restless high school kids that day at Nick's school. He delivered a compelling message about the power of faith and the importance of the choices we make. Reggie told the students that he'd been born to an eighteen-year-old teen prostitute who had been living with her three children in a chicken coop before becoming pregnant with him. She considered having an abortion before turning to a kind high school English teacher who had helped her in the past.

The teacher, Mrs. Dabbs, took in the pregnant teen, and then she and her husband eventually adopted Reggie and raised him, even though they'd already raised six children of their own. Reggie learned of his real mother when he was in grade school, and he spent many years feeling lost until a Christian minister told him that he was a child of God and would always be loved by his heavenly Father.

I can't speak for Reggie's impact on the other kids, but he definitely inspired Nick with another straightforward message: "You can't change your past, but you can change your future."

FINDING A PATH

These are two very powerful points that every child should know, especially those with disabilities or special needs: they may have substantial challenges, but they also have the power to make the best of their lives, and they are never alone as long as they have faith and believe that anything is possible.

I believe God brought Reggie into Nick's life to show him a path. Nick had done very little public speaking before he heard Reggie, but his talk that day showed our son that people can have a powerful and positive impact by honestly sharing their life experiences. A short time later, Nick put that lesson into practice while speaking to one of his first big audiences, a group of nearly three hundred teens.

Following Reggie's example, Nick told his own story that day, sharing his experiences and feelings about being born without limbs and his struggle to win acceptance while searching for purpose and meaning. He explained that over time, with the help of his renewed faith and those who loved him, he realized that he had a purpose in life for which he was beautifully made.

"And so are all of you," he told the teens.

At that point in his speech, a girl in the audience broke down sobbing. Nick stopped speaking out of concern for her, but he didn't know what to do. To his surprise, she raised her hand and asked if she could come forward to give him a hug. This had never happened to Nick before.

He invited her to come forward. She wiped her tears away, walked to the front of the room, and embraced him for several minutes. Nearly everyone in the audience, teachers and students included, was teary eyed by then. Nick was close to falling apart himself when the girl whispered in his ear, "Nobody has ever told me that I'm beautiful the way I am. No one has ever said they love me," she said. "You've changed my life, and you are a beautiful person too."

In his speeches and books, Nick often talks about this as a life-changing moment for him. He'd seen Reggie Dabbs move an audience to tears while also inspiring them, but when the teenage girl hugged him and said that Nick had changed her life, my son realized that he could have that same powerful impact.

Nick had found his purpose in life, the path God had meant for him to follow on this earth. Suddenly everything made sense to him—even his lack of limbs. He realized that God had given him a body that made a powerful statement before anyone even heard him speak.

When people see Nick for the first time, they know immediately that he has dealt with incredible challenges in life. Then when they see him smile, radiating strength, warmth, and optimism, they know Nick has risen above those challenges. They understand without hearing a word from his mouth that Nick has something of value to share.

DOUBTING DAD

Now it is time for me to confess that I was a little slow to jump on board with Nick's plan to become an inspirational speaker. I couldn't see how my son would ever be able to support himself in that role. From what little I knew about Reggie Dabbs, it seemed that he had to travel all over the world to find work. I couldn't imagine my son hauling his wheelchair onto airplanes, buses, and trains to do the same. Constant travel would just be too hard for him.

I'm the dad, after all, and we can be notoriously slow on the uptake when it comes to our children and their ability to rise above our expectations. We tend to be more cautious and conservative because we don't want our kids to struggle. When Nick said he wanted to be a professional speaker, my response was, "What will you speak about?"

His answer didn't exactly fill me with confidence: "I don't know yet."

I didn't want to pour water on the flames of his passion, but I couldn't see how Nick could possibly line up enough paid speaking engagements to pay the bills as an adult. I didn't scoff at his idea, but I did insist that he continue his education and earn a degree in business or accounting so he'd have a backup plan if his public-speaking dreams didn't pan out.

I was locked into the traditional way of thinking about finding a job. Nick had an aptitude for math, but he had a passion for speaking. We compromised. He agreed to pursue double degrees in financial planning and accounting while also speaking in his free time.

I was happy to have Nick enrolled in university. I knew he was doing some speaking too, but I didn't realize he was really serious about it until a gentleman, John Hyman, who identified himself as my son's speaking coach, showed up at our house. I have to admit this was a wise move on Nick's part. If you've ever watched a typical topnotch veteran speaker deliver a speech, you've noticed there is a lot of movement—walking around the stage, waving the arms, and hand gestures. Nick had to learn to hold the attention of his audience with only his tone of voice and his almost superhuman ability to make eye contact with nearly everyone in the audience during his speeches.

GROWING AMBITIONS

Parents often fail to recognize the blossoming ambitions within their children. This is probably because we spent years dragging them out of bed on school days and then nagging them to finish their homework. Moms and dads get it in their heads that they have to do everything for their kids, and they hold on to that notion even as their children mature and begin to find their own motivations. I've heard other parents say they were surprised to discover that their slacker kids had grown into hardworking, driven, and highly focused adults. They didn't know their kids had it in them!

We'd always said that once Nick started talking as a baby, there was no stopping him, and that proved true in his speaking career as well. Nick surprised me with his ambition and drive to become a polished speaker. He took every speaking engagement he could find. He also invited himself to speak whether people wanted to hear him or not. In the early days Nick did not get paid for most of his speaking engagements. He wasn't interested in making money. His goal was to gain experience, hone his skills, and learn his craft. During his university days, he did manage to pick up more and more paid speaking engagements, and we encouraged him to save his earnings so that he could buy a house one day.

Just before he turned twenty, Nick managed to put together a down payment on a small rental property. He even had twenty thousand dollars remaining. We were proud of him because he'd worked hard for that money, booking appearances all over the country.

One of the primary reasons I thought a speaking career wasn't a good choice for Nick was the fact that he would not be able to drive himself to engagements. Dushka and I were busy with jobs and taking care of family matters. I didn't see how Nick would get about, but he figured it out.

I don't recall how long it took me to realize that as soon as Aaron obtained his driver's license, Nick put him on the payroll as his driver. Actually, I'm not sure Nick even paid Aaron, but there must have been some payoff for all the miles he drove, because they ended up going all over Australia together. Little did I know that my sons had hatched even bigger travel plans.

As Nick approached his twentieth birthday, he announced one day that he was going to South Africa, where he intended to use the twenty thousand dollars in his savings account to buy supplies for needy children in orphanages. And if that wasn't stunning enough, Nick told us that he was taking his younger brother with him.

Life with Nick had never been dull, but this was one whopper of a surprise, a triple-header in fact.

South Africa?

All your savings?

Your little brother?

Dushka and I had friends who had lived in South Africa, and we knew it wasn't the most hospitable place in the world. At that point Nelson Mandela had been freed and negotiations to end apartheid were beginning, but there was still a great amount of turmoil, including violent gun battles between protestors and the authorities.

"Why South Africa?" we asked Nick.

Again, his answer did not do much to ease our alarm. Nick said he was answering the call of someone he had never met—a man who said South Africa needed to hear his message. This South African fellow, John Pingo, had contacted Nick on the Internet after seeing one of his videos online. John was active in a Christian ministry in his native country. He was inspired by Nick's video and offered to set up a South Africa speaking tour for him. Most of the engagements were in churches, schools, and orphanages, but some were in prisons!

A Giving Heart

Nick had agreed to do the speaking tour without consulting us. He and John had been communicating online for several weeks, and Nick was so touched by John's stories of needy orphans that he'd decided to use all his savings to help them.

"Do you have to give *all* of it away?" I asked.

"Well, Dad, you and Mum always taught us that it's better to give than to receive, so that's what I'm going to do," he said.

Oh boy! There are many Bible lessons you want your children to take to heart, but sometimes you'd like to tack on an addendum just as a matter of practicality. For instance, I wished we'd taught Nick that it is better to give than receive—as long as you also stash away enough to live on.

We tried to instill kindness and charity as values in all our children. We stressed that they needed to build solid foundations so they could freely share their blessings with others. We wanted them to be responsible citizens and generous spirits. True to his dynamic nature, Nick took this and ran with it.

We were grateful that Nick had a charitable heart and wanted to help others, but we didn't want him to put his own financial stability in jeopardy. Nick reminded me, of course, that I'd often talked about Jesus the Giver, who had given up His own life for us.

"I'm just doing what you taught me to do," he said.

Dushka and I tried to convince Nick that we were all for him being charitable, but he also had a responsibility to cover his own living expenses and support himself.

"You don't want to end up needing charity yourself, Nick. Even if you sell the rental property and give everything you own, you will never satisfy all the need in the world, so it would be better and wiser to use a few thousand dollars of your savings to help the orphans, while keeping enough to help yourself."

I tried to convince Nick that the Christian thing to do was to contribute to others while making sure you could carry your own weight so you didn't become a burden on society. I pointed out that in the Scriptures, the apostle

Paul said we should work to give to others while making sure we have enough for ourselves.

Of course Nick could easily have countered with a quotation from Luke 6:38, "Give, and it will be given to you. . . . For with the measure you use, it will be measured to you," and Matthew 19:21, "If you want to be perfect, go, sell your possessions and give to the poor, and you will have treasure in heaven. Then come, follow me."

Then he might have followed with Proverbs 11:24–25: "One gives freely, yet grows all the richer; another withholds what he should give, and only suffers want. Whoever brings blessing will be enriched, and one who waters will himself be watered."

And he could have finished with a word from 2 Corinthians 9:7: "Each one must give as he has decided in his heart, not reluctantly or under compulsion, for God loves a cheerful giver."

The Bible tells us to teach our children, but in this case, I worried that maybe we did much too good a job. Nick was convinced that giving away all his savings was the right thing to do. He assured us that he would be able to replenish his bank account with more speaking engagements upon his return from South Africa.

AFRICAN ADVENTURE

Honestly, Dushka and I didn't have the energy to fight Nick on his decision to go to South Africa and give his money to charity, because we were even more concerned about safety and his plans to take Aaron with him. Nick also had asked two of his older cousins to accompany and assist him, but one of them had dropped out. Nick said he needed Aaron's help.

Aaron was a very supportive brother who helped Nick get around and served as his caregiver for speaking engagements. He could do the same thing on this adventure to South Africa, Nick said. My point was that while Nick was an adult with a career, his little brother had just turned eighteen and was still in school and living at home. How could we let them both go off to South Africa on a tour arranged by someone we'd never met?

"Who is this John Pingo anyway?" we asked Nick.

Nick gave me John's phone number and said he would answer any of my questions and concerns. I spoke with John, and he sounded very mature and well organized. He was so committed to this speaking tour that he'd sold his car to help finance their travel and to contribute his own donations to the needy. He promised me repeatedly that Nick and Aaron would always be safe, sheltered, and well fed.

Next I spoke to Aaron, who admitted that he was wary at first when Nick suggested the trip to South Africa. In fact his initial response was to reject the idea: "I don't want to be eaten by a lion!"

Once he overcame concerns about becoming snack food for a predator, Aaron became quite enthusiastic about accompanying Nick. Dushka and I did not share that enthusiasm, but we couldn't deny our sons this opportunity.

After Nick and John Pingo promised me they would be safe and that they would both look after Aaron, Dushka and I let them go. We had many misgivings and neither of us slept much while they were gone. It was difficult to stay in communication with them because they were traveling in many areas without cell, or even regular, phone service. They traveled to engagements in Cape Town, Pretoria, Johannesburg, and all points in between riding in a van borrowed from John's aunt.

Dushka and I might have slept even worse during their South African adventure if we'd known that John Pingo wasn't quite as experienced as we had assumed.

THE EMPTY NEST

Parents grow accustomed to being in control of their children and making decisions for them. Once our children reach the age of adulthood, they want to make their own decisions. It's difficult for parents to let go and even harder for them to see their children make mistakes. We can only hope that they learn from their mistakes and from what we've taught them. We have to give them room to fly on their own, even if it's difficult to watch them struggle at first. The hope is that one day they will soar.

We reluctantly allowed Nick to go to South Africa for that reason. He was legally an adult. We were less comfortable with him taking Aaron. In fact, I told Nick that if anything bad happened to his little brother under his care, I would never forgive him. Dushka and I fretted the whole time they were gone, especially if a couple of days passed without hearing from them.

Thankfully they survived their declarations of independence and all the dangers of South Africa. They arrived back home as scheduled two weeks after they departed. Both said their lives were changed by the poverty and hunger they witnessed and also by the ability of those living in such conditions to still be joyful and grateful for their blessings. Our sons did their part to ease the suffering by giving away all Nick's savings. It was hard to be upset with them because they spent the money on needed supplies, appliances, athletic equipment, and gifts for the orphanages and their children. They had many adventures on the trip, and I'm sure we still haven't heard about the most perilous escapades and close calls.

I was thrown for a loop when they confessed that John Pingo turned out to be only nineteen years old. Like me, Nick and Aaron had assumed John was in his late twenties, if not his thirties, because he sounded so mature on the telephone. They discovered that his maturity was hard earned.

John had grown up on a livestock farm in the republic of the Orange Free

State in southern South Africa. He'd run with a bad crowd earlier in life but had become an avid Christian and even owned a small trucking company. John considered the speaking tour he arranged for Nick to be his gift of love to the neediest in his nation. Thankfully he proved to be a reliable organizer and guide, and we are still friends with him and his family.

GRAND AMBITIONS

When Nick took wing, he didn't take the safe route, and that's pretty much been his flight pattern ever since. He's dared to go to some of the world's most dangerous places, including violent prisons in South America, sex-slave shantytowns, and the wretched slums of Mumbai, where he just missed the lethal bombings that killed twenty and injured one hundred or more.

Aaron told me that after they arrived in South Africa on that first trip and drove into Johannesburg, he spotted a sign that said Smash and Grab Area. Aaron asked John what the sign meant, and he explained, "It means this is an area where they will smash your car windows, grab your things out of the car, and run off." The next sound they heard was that of the doors being locked on their van. But they did not turn back.

Dushka and I thought Nick might find the challenges of travel to be too much for him. As parents, we want to protect our children when they go out into the world. Sometimes we see them taking on too much, and we want them to scale back, be more realistic, and ease the burden.

We kept imagining how wearing the travel must be for him. It would be draining on anyone to journey into remote regions with few resources and poor accommodations. Imagine doing it without arms and legs, unable to swat at biting insects or simply drink from a bottle when you are thirsty. Even riding for long periods in vehicles or on airplanes is more difficult for Nick because of his back problems. He's been known to stretch out in the overhead compartments of some airplanes, but only as a joke to scare any fellow passengers who open the door to find him.

We wondered if Nick might return feeling exhausted and overwhelmed by his effort to inspire hope and faith in parts of the world where poverty and despair were so prevalent. Would he see that his twenty thousand dollars was a pitiful amount when compared to the level of need? Would he return to us discouraged and give up on his dream?

No, that did not happen. Nick returned to us physically exhausted but spiritually exalted. He and Aaron were captivated by South Africa and its irrepressible people. Amid the aching poverty, wretched living conditions, sickness, and malnutrition, they were amazed to find so much laughter, joy, singing, and faith. They loved the people's spontaneous singing and African-style choruses. To see those poor children and teenagers happy and singing in spite of all the lack and dire circumstances was something that blew them away. Nick had gone to South Africa to inspire hope in its people, and he returned inspired by the strength and resilience of the human spirit.

LAUNCH TIME

Every parent knows that one day their children must strike out on their own. It's funny because as much as we worry about that day coming, we may have even greater concerns that they will never leave or will keep boomeranging back to us! Parents of disabled and special-needs kids have a much more complicated view on this, of course.

Dushka and I are extremely grateful, and we thank God often, that Nick grew up to be fully capable of supporting himself and his family. There are many parents whose children have more severe disabilities that make it much more difficult, if not impossible, for them to achieve independence. We can only do our best to provide for them, leaning on our faith and whatever support is available.

As you likely know, Nick travels constantly in his career as a speaker and evangelist. The last time I asked, he'd been in at least forty-four countries. A couple of years ago he went on a tour that hit twenty-four countries in twelve months. He has inspired millions of people around the world and brought thousands forth to declare themselves Christians.

We gave our son roots planted in faith and family. He took wing on his own limitless and unstoppable determination. Dushka and I would like to take all the credit, but we all know that Nick's incredible journey has been designed and guided by our heavenly Father. We have planted and others have watered, but the Bible says "it was God who made it grow." I still find it truly remarkable that our child born without limbs has grown into a man who leads people around the world on their walk with God.

TAKEAWAY THOUGHTS

- Perhaps the greatest gifts we can give our children toward their success in adulthood are a foundation of unconditional love, a sense that they have a purpose in this world, a value system to guide them, and a spiritual base as a perpetual source of hope.
- Parents of special-needs children often take it day by day in their kids' younger years because that's the only way they can function. That may well be the appropriate strategy, but once their children reach the teen years, parents should begin to look at whether and to what extent their kids can become independent and self-supporting as adults—and help them prepare for that stage of life.

- Adult children with autism, major mental and physical disabilities, and Down syndrome may be incapable of living independently, so parents must do whatever they can to ensure their children are protected and supported in their adult years by consulting with their physicians, therapists, teachers, and lawyers to determine their capabilities and vulnerabilities.
- No parent wants to put limitations on a child, so if your child identifies a career path that seems overly ambitious or beyond reach, it might work best to guide him to develop a backup plan and help him pick up the necessary skills and knowledge.
- Prepare yourself for the day when your child declares independence and takes flight. The adult you raised just might amaze you.

Nine

Growing Together
Not Apart

Keep the Bonds
of Marriage Strong

While traveling with Nick in Florida a few years ago, we met a young couple whose year-old child was born without limbs. The parents were fans of my son's videos and books. We immediately felt a bond with them. As I talked with them about the challenges of raising such a child, I realized that the husband and wife were exactly the same ages—twenty-six and twenty-eight—that Dushka and I had been when Nick was born. I noted that they seemed to be doing much better than we did at that early stage as parents of a limbless child. They explained that their journey was different from ours in two critical ways.

Early in her pregnancy, the wife underwent an ultrasound, and her doctor recognized that their baby had not developed limbs. Their physician advised them that they might want to consider aborting this baby because of that disability, but they refused. While awaiting the birth of their child, they had time to go through grief and reach acceptance.

The second difference between us was the fact that they had a role model for raising their son—us. The couple said they decided to raise their child because of what they'd learned about Nick through his videos, speeches, and books. Nick gave them hope. Because of him they realized it was possible for their child to have a good and productive life.

Dushka and I are grateful that our perfectly imperfect son's example helped that couple prepare themselves to bring their boy into the world. In the same way, we hope that our experiences raising Nick can help others parent disabled kids.

So far in this book, I've chronicled many of the trials we faced with Nick. I've explained the emotions we felt and the solutions we found. In this chapter, I want to shift the focus from the child to the parents, a child's most valuable assets and greatest advocates.

My basic advice is this: *take care of your child by taking care of your marriage.* The lesson of Matthew 7:24–27 holds true for marriage:

> Therefore everyone who hears these words of mine and puts them into practice is like a wise man who built his house on the rock. The rain came down, the streams rose, and the winds blew and beat against that house; yet it did not fall, because it had its foundation on the rock. But everyone who hears these words of mine and does not put them into practice is like a foolish man who built his house on sand. The rain came down, the streams rose, and the winds blew and beat against that house, and it fell with a great crash.

I've offered abundant testimony to the rains and winds that blew and beat against our marriage in Nick's first few years and beyond. Financial pressures, health concerns, and the 24/7 responsibilities of protecting and nurturing a special-needs child are among the many potentially destructive forces that can tear at the fabric of your relationship. To give a disabled child all the parental care and support needed, you must take care of your marriage and maintain its foundation in rock rather than sand. Marriages and relationships can crumble under the stress of parenting disabled children. Guilt, blame, anger, mistrust, and misunderstandings will fracture all that you've built if you don't find ways to work together rather than falling apart.

It helps to keep in mind that individuals respond to crises in their own ways based on their backgrounds, experience, and brain chemistry, among other complexities. Husbands and wives may have conflicting strategies, contrasting emotional responses, unequal levels of commitment, and disparate breaking points. Those differences can add to the stress unless you focus instead on what you have in common—the welfare of your child and the bonds of your marriage.

Dushka and I went through many difficult stretches, to be certain. Honestly, I've done my best to banish those memories from my mind. The important thing is that our marriage survived, and today we are reaping wonderful rewards. Our family is intact and loving, and we are having the best times of our lives together.

PERFECTLY IMPERFECT PARENTS

People have often said to us over the years, "You must be proud of your son, and you must be special parents." Yes, we are extremely proud of Nick, his achievements, attitude, faith, and positive outlook on life, but we aren't special in any way. We are a middle-class family from immigrant stock. Our greatest asset is one that all people of faith share. Dushka noted this fact during an interview with a reporter doing a story on Nick and his family: "We did the best we could with what we knew. In fact, we did all that any other parent would have done in a given circumstance. The truth is, God did it, and not us."

When Nick was born, I questioned God and His love. I was human, not superhuman; in fact, I was ordinary, maybe even less than that. I did not feel strong. I felt weak. So you can imagine my skepticism at a statement made by a friend when Nick was about two years old.

"Nick could not have been born to a better couple," she said.

She intended that as a compliment, meaning that Dushka and I appeared to be up to the challenges of raising a severely disabled child. We certainly did not see ourselves as the best sort of people for raising such a child.

As life propelled us forward, we felt burdened and blessed at the same time. We were burdened not by Nick but by our doubts and our fear that we were not capable of giving him all that he needed to succeed. And we were blessed to have a son with such a soaring spirit and a marriage that, while only five years old, was built on rock, not sand. We had strong bonds that were not easily broken. They were tested, to be sure, but they held up. We needed each other to give our son the best care and the best childhood possible. We felt that we had to work as hard at keeping our marriage strong as we did at providing for our son.

We've known many single parents who do a wonderful job with their children. They make many sacrifices and endure hardships and loneliness to give their children what they need. Most single parents are heroic people doing their best for their children. Yet most freely admit that it would have been an easier job if they'd had a spouse to help share the load.

Mothers and fathers may have different parenting styles, but each of them is a major influence in a child's life. In fact, fathers probably haven't received the respect they deserve as nurturers rather than simply providers. A recent review of more than thirty-five studies around the world, involving more than ten thousand children, found that fathers and mothers each play critical roles in the personality development of a child. The lack of either can damage a child's emotional and mental health into adulthood, according to a report in the journal *Personality and Social Psychology Review.*

The research found that a father's input is particularly important for behavior and can influence whether a child later tends to drink to excess, take drugs, or suffer mental health problems. This is yet another reason it is so critical for couples to support each other and to stay united when faced with the challenges of parenting disabled and special-needs children.

By the time Nick reached the age of two, we had stopped trying to figure out the *whys* of our son's disabilities. We focused instead on the *hows* of raising him. These were stressful times. It helped that we had five years of relative calm as a married couple before Nick arrived.

The first child always tests the bonds of a relationship, and having a severely disabled child multiplies the stress exponentially. The stress eased a bit once we settled in with Nick at home. As an infant, he was like any other baby in diapers and unable to feed himself, so that gave us a quieter period of adjustment. We embraced the normalcy and basked in it. Eventually Dushka and I poked fun at ourselves at the idea of us being perfectly suited to raise Nick. It became a running joke, usually dipped in irony whenever we hit a particularly rough time or encountered a big challenge. We'd say, "*This* could not have happened to a better couple."

Usually we'd laugh, but often the feeling was bittersweet. Every parent with a special-needs child will tell you that it is an emotional roller coaster. The stress can batter a marriage into numbness. It can drive couples apart. Yet there is also the opportunity to strengthen bonds so they are resilient and strong enough to hold through any challenge and last a lifetime.

SIX STRATEGIES FOR A MARRIAGE UNDER STRESS

When Dushka and I reflect on how we held our relationship together through the challenges of raising Nick and our other children, we can identify a few things that were helpful. There is no guarantee, of course, that they will work for everyone. I've noted before that many parents with disabled and special-needs kids face far greater challenges than we dealt with in raising Nick. We stand in awe of the incredible strength, patience, and heroic efforts of those whose children have more severe physical or mental disabilities. That said, it's probably true that these suggestions can bring some benefits for any couple dealing with stressful parenting situations.

I can't say that we consciously did most of these things, and we certainly had lapses from time to time in sticking with them. Life has a way of distracting you from your best intentions. I've had to reflect on what worked and didn't work to identify each of them. Honestly, most simply came to us after a lot of trial-and-error experiences. Whenever we found something that worked, we stuck with it and tried to be consistent. You may find some of these helpful in your own efforts to keep the relationship bonds strong while facing parenting challenges of your own.

Our relationship while parenting Nick benefitted from these strategies:

1. Developing a Team Nick approach in which we each took on specific roles while sharing responsibilities and supporting each other.
2. Trying to be flexible and adaptable in our parenting roles.
3. Doing our best to always communicate feelings and concerns before problems could occur.
4. Keeping in mind why we married in the first place and taking time to refresh and build upon our bonds.
5. Making the most of all available resources, including family, friends, and ministers; local, state, and federal agencies; professional therapists; support groups; and reliable online sites.
6. Remembering to be grateful and to laugh whenever possible to lighten the load.

Let's look at each of these methods individually.

1. Team Nick

When a child has special needs, parents can easily feel overwhelmed by even the routine daily care required. Stress only increases if they dwell on the unanswerable what-ifs of the future and the challenges awaiting the child in adulthood. Parents easily can fall into despair and depression unless they support each other, take things as they come, do only what can be done, and remain focused on solutions rather than problems.

Every marriage and strong relationship requires a degree of selflessness, giving up the "me" to the "we." Nick's disabilities made it necessary to take it a step further, giving up the "we" for the "us." We became Team Nick, focused on his care and development, but we also did our best to stay close as a couple by spending time together and sharing our feelings.

This situation changed over time, of course, and that is an important point for parents of newborns or young children to keep in mind. Your first years are generally the most difficult because of all the emotional issues, as well as the difficult learning curve and the impact on your lifestyle. Take heart in the fact that as you settle into a routine and a more normal day-to-day existence, the stress will generally subside. You will get better at parenting your child. Don't feel like you have to be perfect or know exactly what to do all the time. Be as patient with yourself and with your spouse as you are with your child.

Working Together

When Dushka became pregnant after five years of marriage, we knew we were in for some major changes, but we had not factored in the impact of a child without limbs. If either of us had remained for long in the initial wave of self-pity and victimization, our relationship might have disintegrated. That didn't happen, in part because we both came from immigrant backgrounds. Our parents and grandparents had struggled mightily and endured great hardships. They had no tolerance for weakness. They made it clear from the beginning that they were on Team Nick, and so it began.

They fortified us. Dushka and I came together and worked as partners with shared goals. We supported each other in caring for our son and dealing with medical specialists, equipment, expenses, therapies, insurance, and schooling. We adjusted our careers and our work schedules so that one of us was always with Nick in his early years of dependence.

Our similar economic backgrounds were a benefit. We were from low-income families and accustomed to life in the slow lane. Dushka did not demand a McMansion. I was okay with driving an economy car. We had always lived within our limited means, and when Nick came along, those limits tightened. Our pie had only so many pieces. Nick's needs became our shared priority.

Selflessness can sometimes seem like a lost concept in a world inundated with selfies, but putting your child and your spouse above yourself is the best way to keep your family united and strong. Christians are called upon to be the light of the world and to look to Jesus, who was willing to give His life for our sins, as a moral guide. He told us to love others as we love ourselves. If all humanity embraced this principle, the world would be a much better and safer place. But at the very least we can apply this principle to our children and to our spouses as well.

Dushka and I may never have achieved complete selflessness when we formed Team Nick, but striving to serve each other first helped us to stay strong in our efforts to give our son all that he needed.

Our family team expanded to include Aaron and Michelle when they arrived, and Nick joined in as we supported and helped each other. We were not the ideal family by any means. We were and remain imperfect. Yet we are united as a family, supportive of each other, and ready to help out when needed, just as my parents and grandparents helped us with Nick. This family tradition of serving others will live on with our three children, all of whom have giving hearts, and my wife and I are grateful to see them sharing their gifts and making a difference.

2. Parenting Without Borders

To reduce conflict as we dealt with the stress of raising a disabled child, Dushka and I had to let go of any traditional concepts we had about the parenting role of the father and the parenting role of the mother. In other words, we had to become parents without borders.

This wasn't all that difficult for us because we'd both been working outside the home, so we were already accustomed to sharing the load when it came to housework, shopping, and meals. When Nick came along, we created a new routine of shared responsibilities, although Dushka definitely was the authority on matters of health and childcare. I never knew why he was crying. She always did.

We learned quickly that caring for Nick required us both to pitch in and do whatever was necessary to keep him safe, healthy, and in the best possible environment. I could not be the traditional old-school father like my father and father-in-law who worked nine to five and expected their wives to serve them meals, do the laundry, and keep the house clean without assistance from them. Dushka could not stick with her full-time job of working as a nurse and midwife while a nanny or day-care center or family member looked after baby Nick.

We both had to toss out those expectations and adjust to parenting Nick in shifts, being flexible in our roles and supporting each other. The need for this became most obvious when Nick came home from the hospital with colic. Later, long after Nick was over the colic, Dushka worked part-time on the night shift at a hospital, so we again had to be flexible in our parenting roles. This wasn't easy, but there was no other way to make it work. We needed Dushka's income to help with the mortgage, as well as living, medical, and other expenses, and our son needed someone with him at all times. So we supported each other and did what we had to do.

Once all the kids were out of diapers, Dushka went back to working full time on rotating shifts. It was tough on her and not great for the kids, although we had support from our parents. We realized, however, that it didn't make sense, even financially, for her to be working so hard outside the home. When we looked at our taxes, we determined that if she cut back to working four days a week, it wouldn't affect our after-tax income that much because the lost income would leave us in a lower tax bracket.

So she changed her schedule to a four-day workweek, which reduced her stress and gave her more time with the kids. Dushka loved nursing, and she could have continued her full-time career if we'd asked our parents to help out more or hired sitters. Instead, she made the kids her priority. We cut back on expenditures and our lifestyle so that Nick, as well as Aaron and Michelle, would have her around more.

In the same way, when Nick was born I stopped pursuing an accounting degree so I could help out in his first few years. Later I went back to school while also working full time so I could get that degree and a better job. We both made adjustments. We had to be flexible. If either of us had refused to make those adjustments, I'm sure there would have been conflicts and turmoil in our relationship.

Playing to Your Strengths

Parenting without borders also means making the most of each partner's strengths without regard to traditional husband and wife roles. If, for example, the wife is a certified public accountant and the husband has to travel all the time, it makes more sense for her to manage the family's finances. In our case, Dushka had an abundance of medical training and experience so she became Nick's chief advocate in that department. I let her handle those things and gave her assistance when she needed me. Major decisions were shared, of course, but often I deferred to her expertise.

It would have been foolish for me, and potentially harmful for Nick, if I insisted that I was "the man of the house" and tried to overrule her in medical matters. We found a balance in our parenting roles that wasn't based on ego or gender but on need and our individual strengths.

3. Talking It Out

As with any relationship that is under stress, communication is essential for parents of special-needs children. If something is bothering you, expressing it right away will help ensure that the issue doesn't cause a meltdown. There is a real temptation to blame your spouse when something goes wrong, but that generally leads only to more conflict. It does no good to lay blame. It's far more important—and healing—to talk it through, come to an agreement on a solution, and then work together to implement it.

Dushka and I find that the longer we're together, the more we can communicate and resolve problems without a lot of discussion. We just know each other so well after nearly forty years of marriage. In our early days together, we learned to talk through issues because so many important decisions had to be made regarding Nick's medical care, his education, our schedules at home and at work, and our bills and budgets. We also moved quite a bit, and that is always a stressful thing that requires extensive planning, adjustments, and coordination.

Faith-Healing Debate

Perhaps our biggest conflict in those early years with Nick was about an issue related to our faith, which was unusual because we both grew up in the same church and we are equally yoked in the commitment we have to our Christian beliefs. I wouldn't say this issue ever threatened our marriage, but we did have intense discussions about it because we both had strong feelings. This is also a matter of debate among other families with disabled children.

From Nick's birth we all prayed and fasted, asking God for a miracle that would give him limbs. When those prayers were not answered, we wondered if it was because our faith was lacking or if God had another plan yet unrevealed.

We believed in God's healing power, and that led to discussions on whether we should look to churches and ministers who were believed to be conduits of that power. Our own church did not offer that. My position was that if God wanted to give our son limbs, He could and would do it irrespective of the place or church affiliation and without relying on an earthly intermediary. Dushka believed it couldn't hurt to try to find a healer anywhere we could. She made a strong argument on several occasions that I wasn't being open minded and that we could be missing opportunities that would benefit Nick enormously.

Faith healing—also known as divine healing, miracle healing, and supernatural healing—has long been a controversy among Christians and other religions. It has split churches and driven believers from one denomination to another. Some believe in faith healing, others hold that only God can perform miracles, and still others are of the mind that miracles on earth ended with the passing of the original apostles.

The Bible has accounts of healings performed by Jesus as well as by Elijah, the apostle Paul, and many others. The Bible says Jesus sometimes refused to perform miraculous healing because He felt the individuals lacked faith in Him and He didn't want to impose it upon them.

Some faiths don't endorse faith healing but do believe in the power of prayer as a healing source in modern times. Others believe that God will heal people through ministers in ceremonies involving the laying of hands on disabled or sick individuals. Dushka and I had many discussions on this topic during Nick's childhood.

I understood that she was acting out of a mother's love for her son. I loved Nick too, but I was not comfortable hopping from one church to the other in hopes of finding a miracle. My wife and others in our family who supported her in this were willing to try for Nick's sake. "How do you know it won't work if you don't take him and try it?" she asked.

Again, I believed that if God's plan was to perform a miracle to heal Nick, He would do it at any place. When Jesus talked with the Samaritan woman at the well, she asked if it was better to worship in Jerusalem or at the mountain. Jesus said the time had come for true believers to pray and worship in every place. He also said when we pray, we are not to make a spectacle of it to draw the attention of people but rather to pray in private behind closed doors. Jesus added that the Father who sees what is done in secret will reward us.

I believe that God can answer our prayers anywhere we are. He is not bound by time and space, and He does not need an intermediary. It didn't help my position that we often had people saying they knew of other churches or missions abroad where miracle healings were occurring.

There were a few faith-healing ministries on television at the time, which caught Dushka's attention with their claims. I contended that God's power was not a media spectacle. He is not about making a show of His healing and forgiveness.

As an adult, Nick has traveled throughout the world. He has been prayed for by many who would like to see him with arms and legs, yet he remains without limbs. Even so, he has found a life of purpose.

Spiritual Healing Comes First

Within a few years, I came to believe strongly that we needed to come to terms with the reality of Nick's disabilities and move on. If God decided to heal him, He would do it on His schedule, not ours. I also saw that there was such need in the world and so many others who lacked limbs or had lost them. How could God choose to heal only Nick when so many others had physical problems like his or far worse?

We tend to forget that God is more concerned about our spiritual well-being than our physical health. This is illustrated in Scripture when Jesus was visiting a home and a crowd surrounded it. Some friends brought a crippled man on a mat to be healed, and the only way they could get him to Jesus was to lower him through an opening in the roof.

The first thing Jesus did was to tell the man his sins were forgiven. In the mind of Jesus, that was the greatest gift He could give because it meant this man had the opportunity to spend eternity in heaven. When some of those present questioned Him, Jesus said, "Which is easier: to say to this paralyzed man, 'Your sins are forgiven,' or to say, 'Get up, take your mat and walk'? But I want you to know that the Son of Man has authority on earth to forgive sins." Only then did Jesus say to the crippled man, "Get up, take your mat and go home." The man did as commanded, walking away while everyone watched.

This is why I believe God considers spiritual healing more important than physical healing, and I thought we should give Him time to reveal His plans for Nick without relying on faith healers.

In those early years of Nick's life, I sometimes had strangers come up to me when I was with him and say, "One day God will make him whole." Things like that did not easily sway me. I'm skeptical of faith-healing claims, but I am a believer in God's power. I believe if God wants Nick to have arms and legs, He will provide them one day.

This debate went on for Nick's first couple of years. I respected Dushka's position as a mother who desperately wanted her son to have an easier life. I just thought God would reveal His plan for Nick on His own schedule, and

I didn't want to put him or us through the disappointment of going to many supposed healing places and subjecting Nick to people with their own agendas and motives for promoting themselves as healers.

His miracle has yet to come, but as Nick often says, God has allowed him to be a miracle for millions of others through his inspirational messages of hope and faith. I believe that is the purpose for each one of us, to be the inspiration and the light in our own corners of the world, no matter what circumstances we face. The Bible says that godliness with contentment is great gain and that we must give thanks in everything because that is the will of God in Christ Jesus. This is our role and our challenge.

Our conflicting views on faith healing led to some stressful moments. Our discussions were sometimes contentious and highly emotional. Having a child with disabilities will create pressures like that on a marriage. You have to work through them without attacking or hurting each other. It helps to keep your shared goals and beliefs in mind at all times during such disputes. In the end, we knew that we each had our son's best interests at heart.

4. Keeping Your Love Alive

Caring for a special-needs child often requires 24/7 vigilance, and it stresses a family's resources as well as a couple's relationship. Dushka and I had to carve out time for each other as a couple whenever we could. It wasn't easy, and we weren't always great at rekindling the fires as often as we needed. We realized that to give Nick a proper foundation, we had to be on solid ground with each other. Husbands and wives can get so caught up in raising their children and providing all that the family needs that they neglect the needs of each other.

Taking care of your relationship by remembering and refreshing the love and affection that brought you together in the first place is critical. Your love for each other will strengthen you for loving and caring for your children. Many nights we would go to bed exhausted from caring for Nick when he was a baby. The best thing we could do on those nights was to end them in each other's arms, even if it was just to hold each other until we fell asleep.

Finding time to be present and attentive to each other during the day was often difficult if not impossible, so how we related at night was important for keeping the bonds of our relationship strong. Sometimes couples with special-needs kids become so focused on the children that they feel guilty if they take time for each other. Dushka and I eventually realized that Nick needed his mother and father to be together more than he needed us hovering over him constantly.

We did our best to spend quiet time together each day and to occasionally ask a family member or friend to baby-sit so we could go out and get re-acquainted as a couple. Relationship experts say even just twenty minutes a day can help shore up the foundations of a marriage under stress. Over time the intense passion of a couple's early days together will likely diminish, but even spending a few minutes talking about the initial attraction can reignite those flames.

Take a break from discussing bills and medical issues for twenty minutes or so each day. Hold hands, snuggle, go for a walk, have a romantic dinner. Consider your enduring commitment and affection for each other to be a gift to your children that will keep on giving. In our case this commitment is not only to each other but also to God. The Bible talks about marriage being for life, and we take that seriously. We are accountable to each other and to God, so we make the effort to keep our love alive and our bonds strong.

5. Use the Lifeboats

Ministers and banquet speakers are fond of the oft-told story of the misguided Christian who does not heed warnings of an impending flood because he is certain God will send a miracle if the waters threaten his life. The same believer ends up on the roof of his house, surrounded by rising waters, yet he still turns down offers of escape from would-be rescuers in a canoe, a lifeboat, and a helicopter. Finally the waters engulf and drown him, and he finds himself face to face with God.

"Why didn't You send a miracle?" the believer asks.

God replies, "My poor son, I sent you a warning. I sent you a canoe. I sent you a lifeboat. I sent you a helicopter. What more were you looking for?"

My guess is that this guy was holding out for the angel Gabriel to bring an ark. The lesson is, don't miss the boat while waiting for a miracle. Take help where you can find it. This lesson applies to all people in crises or under intense stress and particularly to parents of disabled and special-needs children.

Dushka and I understand the siege mentality that makes couples want to simply go home, lock the door, turn out the lights, and mourn. We did that for a brief period after Nick was born. We isolated ourselves despite many helping hands reaching out to us. We needed time to wrap our brains around this life-changing development.

Then, after a month or so, we came out of our self-imposed exile, and eventually we welcomed every lifeboat that came our way. We were especially glad for the lifeboats of family and friends, pastors, social workers, therapists, government assistance, medical experts, local service agencies, and anyone who could assist us in helping our son thrive.

We advise other parents dealing with similar challenges to make use of any and all resources available. You are not alone. There are many resources. Don't be too proud to accept help from family members, friends, and others reaching out to you. The Internet puts the world at your door, and while it is advisable to be cautious about the sources you rely on, there is a wealth of valuable information out there.

You might want to begin with your child's doctors and nurses, as well as teachers and school counselors. They can help you tap local and regional agencies and organizations with expertise and experience. The same holds true when seeking to strengthen your marriage or relationship. Don't be afraid to ask for help. It's not a sign of weakness. It takes wisdom and strength to recognize when you are overwhelmed or at a loss for answers.

Dushka and I welcomed counseling from our church pastor, family members, and members of our church. On the financial side, we received wonderful support from many who held fundraisers or contributed money to help Nick. I've mentioned that Dushka's family created a scholarship fund for Nick, and the Lions Club was incredibly helpful in providing wheelchairs and prosthetics. Another great source of assistance was Blue Nurses, a service provided by the Blue Care organization in Australia, which provided volunteer caregivers for Nick when he was studying at the university. He has since done fundraising for their organization to show his gratitude.

Family members also supported us by baby-sitting or helping pick up our kids from school so we could take vacations or steal some time together. We were an average middle-class working couple without many financial resources, so we leaned heavily on family, friends, and others.

Back then we didn't know the term *respite care,* but we certainly knew the concept. It's temporary-relief care service for families of children or adults with special needs. It can range from a few hours of care to overnight or extended periods. You can get respite care from family members, friends, or professional care providers so you and your spouse can get a break, whether it's a movie, a class, a date night, or a vacation.

Dushka and I made the decision not to use full-time caregivers at home because we wanted to have a more normal family life and we wanted Nick to do as much as possible for himself. We all pitched in to help when he needed us. We found that working together brought us closer as a family, and even today with the entire family relocated in California, we feel the same way.

6. Lighten the Load

The Bible teaches us to give thanks in all circumstances. Giving thanks in good times and for beautiful gifts is not that hard. We do it with cheer and excitement, and so it should be. Children are among the greatest gifts, and that includes those who are perfectly imperfect. Parents of these special kids often tell me they've learned so much about courage, perseverance, and love from them. A relationship that has been stressed and endangered can benefit greatly when we remember that our spouses and our children are blessings in our lives.

The Bible tells us that Jesus was struck by the lack of gratitude shown when only one of ten lepers He had cured returned to thank Him. The Son of God knew that gratitude itself can be a healing force. Husbands and wives often forget to apply gratitude to each other. They get caught up in the daily scramble and the many responsibilities of raising a family and forget to thank the person who is always there for them, working alongside them, comforting them, and supporting them.

I'm a work in progress on this front. I've tried to surprise Dushka with gifts, but I'm not the best at picking them out. I usually ask sales clerks and other women for advice and suggestions. Sometimes I even find something she likes! (Though she never complains when I've failed miserably.) I also try to show my gratitude for her with surprise dinners. Sometimes I cook them, and she actually appears to enjoy them, which I'm very grateful for in return.

Dushka once surprised me by planning a special vacation. She spent weeks arranging it, even secretly getting my boss to give me the time off and flying in my sister to watch the kids. I still didn't know of the plan when I went to the airport to pick up my sister and her son, who I thought were just visiting us for a few days. My sister feared that I'd be so overwhelmed when the trip was announced that I might have a heart attack, so she kept asking me if I felt okay on our trip home from the airport.

We began to prepare lunch at home for our visitors when the kids spotted a white stretch limousine coming up the street. We all watched it approach, thinking the driver was lost or looking for a neighbor. When the car parked in front of our house, I was sure the driver had made a mistake. I opened the door, and he said, "I'm looking for Boris!"

Before I could say he must be mistaken, Dushka raced up and revealed the surprise. "We're going to Vanuatu!" This was my dream destination—a South Pacific nation made up of eighty-three beautiful islands featuring tropical rain forests, waterfalls, mountains, and beautiful beaches. Friends of mine had gone there and described it to me, and I'd always wanted to take Dushka so we could see it for ourselves.

Dushka, who does the family financing and balances the checkbook, had already arranged payment for the hotel, not to mention our airline tickets. She simply handed me my passport and my bag already packed. She then revealed that my sister Radmila had come to watch our kids. All I could do was beam with pleasure and thank her profusely—for the rest of our lives. I actually planned a similar surprise trip for her a few years later to an island getaway, so I expressed my gratitude that way too.

These were not extravagant trips, and smaller expressions of gratitude and love are always welcome too. It's the thought that counts, and living with an attitude of gratitude toward each other every day can help a couple overcome many challenges.

Humor is another healing force for married couples. Our kids sometimes tease me about being too serious, and I guess that is often the perception of the father with a lot of responsibilities, but I've relaxed more over the years as they've grown.

Laughter and humor are important in any relationship. Dushka and I were able to retain our sense of humor, and we found that laughter is a wonderful way to relieve the stress and tensions. The Bible tells us to make a joyful noise and to give thanks in all circumstances, and I think that's great marital advice.

Sometimes we didn't know whether to laugh or to cry when difficulties arose, but laughter was usually a more helpful response. It helped that Nick has a great sense of humor too, and his ability to laugh at life draws people to him and helps break down barriers and misconceptions. It's a wonderful gift.

Gratitude is another terrific stress reliever that can be used to reframe almost any situation, casting it in a new light and improving your disposition. Therapists say that the parents of disabled and special-needs kids benefit from focusing on their children's strengths and being grateful for what they can accomplish rather than always being concerned about their disabilities.

Nick often tells the story of a family friend with Down syndrome who told him that it's great to have his disability "because it means you love everybody." Now that is an attitude of gratitude. Such an upbeat and positive approach can also be a wonderful balm for couples who have parenting challenges. Dushka and I developed the habit of looking for the upside and focusing on the good as a way to stay positive in our relationship. For example, it was true that there were additional expenses in raising a child with no limbs, but we softened that blow by noting that we never had to buy Nick a car or shoes or gloves while raising him.

Nick has been known to borrow those lines in his speeches and books, and he loves to play pranks like riding around on the airport baggage carousel and talking to people waiting for their luggage. He also makes jokes while expressing gratitude for the usefulness of "my little chicken leg," which is the nickname Michelle gave his left foot when she was a child.

Proverbs tells us, "A cheerful heart is good medicine, but a crushed spirit dries up the bones." The healing power of laughter and gratitude has been well documented in scientific studies; both laughter and gratitude have the ability to trigger beneficial stress-relieving chemicals in the brain. I encourage all couples to maintain a sense of humor even in the hard times and to always give thanks for the blessings life brings.

TAKEAWAY THOUGHTS

- One of the most harmful things parents of a disabled child can do is to neglect their marriage. Your child needs a solid family foundation of support and love—and you need each other to be sources of strength.
- I've advised you to develop team approaches for your child's medical care and for the school years, but no team is more important than the parental team whose members shoulder responsibilities and offer encouragement and support to each other.
- As traditional as Dushka and I are in our approach to marriage and parenting, we realized early on that we had to be flexible and adaptable in our roles, whether that meant me cooking and cleaning or my wife serving as the disciplinarian and in-house accountant.
- Frustrations and tensions can easily escalate in a household with a special-needs child, so open communication and expressed feelings are vitally important.
- We found it helpful from time to time to go off together and remember why we married in the first place.

- There is no shame in making the most of available resources, including family, friends, ministers, therapists, psychologists, support groups, and government agencies. If you need help to keep your marriage strong, ask for it!
- Laughing at yourselves and life's craziness is a great way to lighten the load. We recommend fun family times, fun friends, and funny movies in large doses.

Ten

A Matter of Faith

Build a Spiritual Foundation

Dushka and I did all we could to prepare Nick for an independent life. We wanted him to be successful, happy, and fulfilled. There was one concern about his future. Nick wanted to marry and have a family, but we weren't sure he'd ever fulfill that dream.

Then, just as Nick was approaching his twenty-eighth birthday, he contacted us on Skype from his home in California. He seemed excited and in a very good mood.

"I have something I want to tell you," he said.

His nervous smile tipped me off, and I blurted out, "You've met a girl!"

Nick's eyes widened and his jaw dropped. "How did you know?"

He thought I'd been reading his mind or spying on him from across the world. I told him it was a father's intuition.

"Well, you're right," he said. "She's wonderful!"

He told us he'd met this Christian girl through a mutual friend in Dallas. Nick then held up a photograph of a young woman with such exotic beauty I couldn't help but blurt out again, "What is her nationality?"

Nick explained that her mother is of Mexican heritage and her father was Japanese.

"Her name is Kanae Miyahara, and while her features are Asian, she grew up in Mexico and speaks Spanish," Nick explained.

Her parents had met when they both worked for a Japanese-owned horticulture company in Mexico. Kanae and her siblings were raised in central Mexico. Kanae had moved to Dallas as a teenager. She was a nursing student and a strong Christian.

Nick told us this and then waited for my usual response whenever he told me about a new girl in his life. In the past, I had not been supportive or enthusiastic. This was mostly because my instinct was always to protect Nick from having his heart broken. Privately I had always harbored doubts about his marriage prospects. I knew it would take a very special woman to marry a man without limbs.

"Well, Dad, I know you must have something negative to say," Nick said, prodding me.

This time I surprised him by saying, "She's beautiful, and I don't have a single negative thing to say about her."

Nick took that as a good sign.

I later told Dushka that my only concern was that this young woman seemed almost too good to be true. Over time, we came to realize that even though Kanae had a very different background from us, there were two major things we had in common. She loved Nick unconditionally, and she believed her faith could help them overcome any obstacles.

FULL CIRCLE

We would later learn that Kanae did not grow up in a Christian household. After a difficult childhood, she found her way and became a Christian when she was fifteen years old. Even though Dushka and I came from strong Christian families and had been Christians all our lives, we came to be inspired by the depth of Kanae's faith. Her love for Nick was equally inspiring, and seeing them come together as a couple, then as husband and wife, and now as a mother and father has brought us full circle in our own journey of faith with Nick.

I know many parents with disabled children, and nearly all of them seem to have struggled early on with questions of faith. The most common is "How could a loving God so cruelly burden one of His children?"

It may help ease your mind to understand that having questions about God and His intentions is a natural part of being a Christian living in a world that includes sin and pain as well as grace and joy. Parents of disabled children who question God in their prayers may feel guilty for doing so, but remember that Jesus did the same in His darkest hour on the cross when He looked to heaven and said, "My God, my God, why have you forsaken me?"

To ask why suffering is allowed is a very natural response and part of the walk of faith for those with special-needs children. We may wonder and never understand what God is trying to teach us or how a child's pain can demonstrate His grace and glory. Romans 8:38–39 says that nothing can separate us from the love of God. When our imperfect lives bring us pain beyond our comprehension, all we can do is remain faithful and surrender to His mercy and love. The question of why bad things happen to good people is always difficult, if not impossible, to answer. Those of faith often have to abandon any hope of understanding and simply rely on their spiritual beliefs. There is no easy answer for anyone with a suffering child.

Some parents who have raised special-needs children say there are re-wards to be derived from the experience, but many also ask if those rewards are worth the high price paid by the child who must struggle through life. Christians generally take the view that our rewards await us in heaven. God does not promise us an easy life on this earth. His own Son paid the highest price of all when He died on the cross for our sins.

I come from a believer's perspective, yet even if Nick's disabilities caused me to deny God and put faith out of my life, Nick would still have no limbs. Faith only helps us view our circumstances and approach them from a Christian perspective of surrender. It does not guarantee solutions or an easy life on earth.

Despite many hours of fasting and prayer by everyone in our family and our church, and even by missionaries in other parts of the world, God did not deliver the miracle we sought for Nick. Instead, we had to move on and live with our son's disability. We chose to believe, as the Bible tells us, that even with an amount of faith the size of a mustard seed, nothing is impossible; we can move mountains.

If we have true faith, God can do anything in our lives. Nick is proof of that. We can see that now. Yet when a child is born with disabilities or special needs, even the most spiritual parents will have questions about God's intentions.

Christians are taught that before Adam and Eve were banished from the Garden of Eden as a result of their sins, there were no sicknesses or disabilities in the world. For that reason, Christians might wonder—as I certainly did—if a less than perfect child is created as some sort of punishment from God for sins committed or for lacking faith. Parents might feel also that God is being unfair to them. Resentment like that can stir anger and doubts about their beliefs.

Dushka and I went through all those negative thoughts and feelings. We learned that a great deal of faith is needed to overcome them. Even more spiritual strength is needed to reach the point of accepting that God doesn't make mistakes. All children are born in His image to know Him and bring Him glory.

Dushka and I had quite a journey before reaching the point of accepting that a disabled child is created to be perfectly imperfect according to the design of our Father in heaven—for the purpose He has in mind. Like the fable of the woman who used her cracked water pot to nurture flowers as she walked with it each day, our imperfections have a purpose. We often can't discover that purpose without first accepting that it exists and then searching to find it.

According to His Purpose

I was a lay minister when Nick was born. Before his birth, I had often preached about God's goodness and His infinite love for us as reflected in Romans 8:28: "And we know that in all things God works for the good of those who love him, who have been called according to his purpose."

After Nick's birth I could imagine members of the congregation thinking, *If this is how God treats good Christians, why would we want to serve such a cruel Father?*

Members of our church were as aggrieved as we were. They joined us in prayer sessions and fasting to ask God for a miraculous restoration of Nick's arms and legs. The Scriptures say God will take care of you and bless you if you obey Him. We felt we'd been obedient to God. We could not understand how a child without limbs could be a reflection of His love. The only thing I could figure out was that God was testing us just as He'd tested others of great faith, such as Job and Joseph in the Old Testament.

I eventually accepted that even the most traumatic events in our lives could lead to joy, fulfillment, happiness, and greater faith. Our experiences with Nick offer proof to other parents with disabled children that God does love them. They are not mistakes. They have purpose.

When bad things happen to us, it isn't necessarily a punishment. How many times have "bad things" that happened to you turned out to be blessings in disguise? Nick's disabilities were certainly perceived to be a bad thing, yet our son has been an incredible blessing. We've had many other examples of this in our lives. That is the reality of life on this earth. Dushka and I had to move beyond our doubts and fears and live in faith. It wasn't always easy, but then again, maybe God didn't want life to be easy for us. Maybe He wanted to test us so that when Nick grew up to be such an inspiring child of God, we would be all the stronger in our faith.

Because of our early struggles and the unanswered questions and prayers, we were blind to Nick's purpose until God revealed it. Without our faith, we might never have been able to guide Nick and prepare him for the life he has today. Our faith gave us strength, motivation, and hope that were essential for Nick's survival and happiness. We remained believers and planted confidence in our Father's goodness in Nick's heart. Today his own faith is the driving force for his purpose.

This same power is available to all who choose to believe. Jesus said, "Apart from me you can do nothing. . . . In this world you will have trouble. But take heart! I have overcome the world." The apostle Paul gained the same strength by believing, "I can do all things through Christ who strengthens me."

In that spirit, Dushka and I wielded our faith as a shield against doubt and fear. We chose to make the most of each day, hoping for the best in the days to come. My wife and I tried not to overanalyze but instead to take hope in Scripture and its positive messages, such as these:

- God sees and knows best.
- He knows why, and I don't have to understand it.
- He says He loves me, and I just have to accept and believe it.
- All things work for the good of those who love God.
- With each new burden, He will provide added strength to enable us to bear it.

We faltered in our faith after Nick's birth, but our son eventually helped make us stronger Christians with his lack of bitterness, his determination, and his unflagging spirit. It was a gradual process. We didn't share our return to faith with others at first. Over time we went public, reading the Bible and praying with our pastor and a few friends. We were still feeling our way, trying to wrap our heads around what it meant to be the Christian parents of a child who had seemed cruelly burdened by his Creator.

We came to a tentative acceptance, but we still had moments of doubt, fear, and confusion. Some questions about Nick's future still haunted us. We couldn't answer them, so we would try to pray them away. The process was like building muscle strength. You keep lifting weights until you fail, growing stronger until you push through to another level. In this case, we were building the strength of our faith even as we prayed and fasted for a miracle.

We took hope from examples in Scripture of God responding to His children seeking healing, including Sarah and Hannah, who were barren until He gave them the miracle of children. Jesus healed many lepers, the deaf, the blind, and the crippled. We're told He brought Lazarus back from the dead. Yet there are examples also of those who were denied miracles because they lacked faith or because God had another purpose for them. Sometimes it seemed He wanted them or those close to them to have greater faith or more patience before they were judged worthy of healing.

King Solomon wrote that life becomes meaningless in the absence of God. When you believe that a new beginning awaits in life after death, the struggle on earth makes more sense. Faith, then, gives meaning to what is beyond our capacity to understand, such as His reasons for allowing His children to suffer disabilities.

Even as we came to terms with being parents to our son without limbs, we grappled with the question of why God would inflict a child with such a burden. Our Bible studies provided some guidance. We're told to rejoice in our sufferings, knowing that they can bring about endurance, which produces character and hope as God's love pours into our hearts through the Holy Spirit (Romans 5:3–5).

We're also told to count it a joy when we meet trials of various kinds (James 1:2), and we're assured that "blessed is the [one] who remains steadfast under trial, for when he has stood the test he will receive the crown of life, which God has promised to those who love him" (James 1:12).

We had to hold on to the thought that while God is loving, kind, and fair, life on this earth can be uncaring, cruel, and unfair. We also had to accept that we are created to bring glory to God, and a disabled child can do that just as easily as a healthy child. God makes no promises that our lives will be pain free; He promises only that He will always be with us if we believe. We realized that we had to trust in His wisdom and good purposes, in His Word rather than in our feelings, and in His grace, which is sufficient for any trial.

The questions for God that dwell in the minds of parents of disabled and special-needs children are relentless. I still struggle even today, though I see that my son has a wonderful life and family and a purpose to inspire hope in people around the world. I still don't fully understand the whys of Nick's disability.

Does my son have to live without arms and legs to fulfill God's purpose? Couldn't he have been just as inspirational as a man with arms and legs? Is it not possible for him to lead thousands to Christ with a normal body?

Even though many questions remain on the table, there is no doubt that our deeply rooted faith has helped my wife and me to better cope with our son's challenges. We know that God is the Potter and we are the clay, and the clay doesn't get to say, "Why did you make me like this?" The Potter decides, and the clay either molds into what He wants or grows brittle and of little use.

Still we continue to hope for a miracle, and so does our son. As I mentioned earlier, Nick keeps shoes in his closet because he is waiting for God to respond to his prayers for arms and legs. His faith is that strong. I'm in awe of its depth even when he faces challenges that would send most people off a cliff.

TLC (The Learning Channel) did a special on Nick called *Born Without Limbs,* which first aired in 2015. There is a segment showing him taking off his T-shirt. He uses his teeth to pull it up to his shoulders; then he pins a bit of the T-shirt against a wall and contorts his body until he can slip his head out of the neck and remove it entirely. The simple act of taking off his shirt requires ten times as much energy and struggle for him than it does for the rest of us. That is his life and his burden, yet most days he bears it with grace and good humor.

My son has certainly surpassed me in the depth of his faith, and I'm grateful. He needs that power to fuel his ambitions and get him through each day.

A Match Made in Heaven

Dushka and I were still living in Australia when Nick began courting Kanae. We didn't meet her face to face until she and Nick had been seeing each other for about three months. We did talk to her and our son on Skype a few times. She was very charming, a lovely young lady. It was obvious that Kanae was quite taken with Nick. She looked at him with such love, and she laughed at everything he said. As his father, I was certain that Nick was not that funny!

I'm teasing, of course, but any parent will agree that we get to know our children for all their talents as well as all their imperfections and faults. Even when they reach adulthood, we still think of them as children. We know them so well that when they find love, we can't help but wonder if the other person really knows what he or she is getting into.

Nick's lack of limbs meant he would be unable to do some things that husbands typically do, like helping to feed and dress their children. He would also need assistance from his wife at mealtime and when bathing and dressing.

This may sound harsh, but I did find myself wondering why Kanae, who could have likely married anyone she wanted to marry, would be willing to spend her life with a man who had no arms and no legs. It wasn't that I didn't think Nick was worthy of love, but we'd had some disappointing experiences with women he'd dated previously, including one whose parents forced a breakup because they didn't want her to marry him.

After Nick had been dating Kanae for a few months and their relationship seemed to be serious, Dushka and I decided to travel to the United States so we could meet her. We wanted a better read on her background, her intentions, and the depth of her faith.

We also wanted to make sure Kanae knew what she was getting into if she married our son. We had no doubt he would be a great husband and father, but being married to someone without limbs would come with certain challenges. Most importantly, we had questions about the depth and strength of Kanae's faith because we knew if she married Nick it would be tested, just as ours was when he was born. My wife and I once had believed our faith could stand any test. Nick's birth and the challenges he faced as a child made us question God's love many times as we raised him. We felt it would take a deeply spiritual woman to be his wife.

As Nick's parents, we knew exactly what he could do for himself and what he needed assistance with. We had come to see that there would be many challenges for anyone who married Nick due to his intense travel schedules, the demands on his time and attention, and even the daily care and assistance he needed. His wife would have to support him, console him, hold him, and give him wise counsel in moments of doubt, despair, and uncertainty.

We had many concerns to discuss with Kanae, but on the deepest level this was about matters of faith. We believed that Kanae was in love with Nick. We wanted to be sure she had the spiritual strength to support and help Nick fulfill whatever his purpose might be.

He had pursued relationships with a few girls over the years, and he'd been hurt when they backed away. Most were well intentioned. These women liked our son and admired him but saw him as a friend rather than as a potential husband. Nick needed a wife who truly accepted him and loved him and would not hurt him or destroy his life by walking away after marriage.

Marriages Built on Faith

We knew a few other disabled people with wonderful and devoted spouses. Among those we'd met were Nick's friend and mentor Joni Eareckson Tada and her husband, Ken. Joni is a quadriplegic and the founder of Joni and Friends, which is a global advocacy group for the disabled. Ken is a retired high school coach and teacher. They married the year Nick was born, in 1982, and they have remained together, traveling the world to serve others with their Christian charity work.

Ken wrote a book explaining how an able-bodied man fell in love with a disabled woman. Their story is quite moving, yet they are also very candid about the many challenges they've gone through. Love can be stretched and stretched until it breaks, especially with the stress of a disabled child or partner. Ken notes that he found it physically exhausting and mentally challenging to be both husband and caregiver to Joni. He has had bouts with depression and dark times when he didn't think the marriage would last. "If it wasn't for the fact that I believed in God, I wasn't sure I was going to make it," he told an interviewer.

Their shared faith and honest communication has helped Ken and Joni weather many storms. They are exceptional people. Ken was a strong Christian when he met Joni, and he has acknowledged that his faith has been tested many times by the stress of their marriage. I was concerned Nick and Kanae might face similar challenges in their marriage, which is another reason we wanted to talk with Kanae before their relationship moved forward. Marriage is a wonderful experience most of the time, yet it can be humbling and difficult as circumstances change, passion diminishes, and harsh reality causes stress and frustration. The bottom line is that a relationship should not be based on mere physical attraction or the desire for marital status. Both spouses have to share basic beliefs and values, and they need to have an enduring commitment to sustain them through the inevitable and often unexpected challenges that life brings.

We wanted Nick to have a wife who was equally committed to their marriage. She had to be fully prepared for a husband who, despite his extraordinary determination and positive attitude, still has many physical challenges.

THE INTERROGATION

That was in our minds when we traveled from Australia to meet Kanae in early 2011. We had serious questions to ask her, but we didn't mean to intimidate her. In retrospect, I can see why she came to humorously describe our little talk with her as the Interrogation. It was her first sit-down with her potential in-laws, and while we weren't confrontational, we did want to make sure that her love and faith were strong enough to sustain a marriage to our son. Kanae was nervous that day, as anyone would be when first sitting down with the potential in-laws. Yet she handled our questions with grace, intelligence, and a surprising level of maturity. We understood where her inner strength came from when she told us about her family background. She and her siblings, who grew up in Mexico and spoke Spanish, were known as "the Japanese family" in their hometown neighborhood because they were the only kids with Asian features. Kanae's parents divorced when she was in her early teens, which caused additional turmoil for her family. Their mother moved out of the home and later to the United States. Kanae and her siblings then lived with her father and helped him run his nursery and landscaping business.

Her father, Kiyoshi Miyahara, was diagnosed with leukemia when Kanae was still in elementary school. He returned to his native Japan for treatment when Kanae was fourteen years old. At that point Kanae took over the care of her younger brother and also ran her father's business while he underwent chemotherapy.

Sadly her father died from the cancer in Japan, which led to Kanae and her siblings eventually moving to the United States, where they joined her mother and other relatives in the Dallas area. Her mother and older sister joined a Christian church there. Kanae began attending and gave her life to Jesus.

As Kanae eloquently shared her story, Dushka and I were impressed. Her delicate beauty and sweet nature belied a quiet strength. Her devotion to her younger brother and plans to become a nurse showed us that she also had a nurturing spirit and a giving heart. When we questioned Kanae about her faith, she was honest in saying that she'd rarely gone to her mother's Catholic church as a girl because she worked in her father's business, and religion was not a focal point for the family.

She had struggled with faith as a teen in Mexico. It was only when she came to the United States and joined her sister's Christian youth group that Kanae found the path that gave her comfort and peace. She said her new-found faith had brought her to Nick because they'd met when he was giving a talk to a small group of Christian friends. Their relationship was forged upon their shared spiritual beliefs.

As compelling as all this information was, Dushka and I asked Kanae many probing questions. She handled them well and made a strong case. Kanae said that upon meeting Nick she looked into his eyes and his heart rather than focusing on his lack of limbs. She explained that she'd been in the process of breaking off a relationship with a longtime boyfriend whose faith was not equally yoked to hers. In our son she saw a man who not only shared her beliefs but also traveled the world to share them with others.

Dushka, who has the practical, no-nonsense manner of a veteran nurse, continued to ask pointed questions. "Do you fully understand how Nick's disabilities impact his daily life? Are you prepared to be with someone who relies on a wheelchair, who cannot give you a lot of help around the house, who needs assistance while eating and using the restroom?"

Kanae was straightforward in her responses. She surprised us by saying she had already assisted Nick in many ways, even lifting him up from the ground and helping him into a wheelchair. The surprising element of that was mostly the fact that Nick is a solid guy and heavier than he looks. We couldn't imagine this wisp of a young woman hoisting him up into his wheelchair. It was hard enough for me to do that.

Perhaps the deciding point in our conversation with Kanae that day was her response to another tough question posed by Dushka. Doctors have never identified a medical, genetic, or environmental reason for Nick's lack of limbs. Several had assured us the odds of him passing it on to his children were astronomical. Even so, Dushka and I needed to know if Kanae was prepared for that possibility, if she had the spiritual foundation to withstand such a major test of faith.

The question Dushka posed to Kanae was this: "What if you and Nick married and you had a child without limbs?" To her credit, Kanae did not flinch in her assured response: "I know there might be a slight possibility of that, but even if we had five kids born like Nick, I'd love them the same as I love him. If that should happen, I also feel I'd be more prepared than most people because Nick would be there to serve as a great example."

Needless to say, Kanae won us over that day. If this was an interrogation, she convinced her interrogators to join her side. If we had any lingering doubts about her having a long-term relationship with Nick, they centered on their very different cultural backgrounds. Those questions were washed away a few months later when we joined Nick and Kanae at her family's home in Dallas.

You might be tempted to think that Serbian Australians have little in common with Japanese Mexican Americans, but you would be wrong in that. Kanae's family had embraced Nick as one of their own. We loved Kanae. And we all loved to laugh, sing, and have a good time. With all those bonds and our shared Christian faith, we figured there was no stopping Nick and Kanae from having a wonderful life together. And they've proved us right.

During the writing of this book, Nick and Kanae welcomed a second son, Dejan, into their family. He is a healthy and rambunctious boy, just like his older brother, Kiyoshi, who is named for Kanae's father.

As I noted earlier, seeing our son now with his wife and two children has brought us full circle in our journey of faith. Nearly all the doubts and fears and worries that shook our faith in Nick's early days have been swept away. We had questioned God's love of Nick. We questioned whether any woman could love and marry him. We wondered if our son would ever have a family of his own.

I've heard it said we sometimes are so focused on asking for the miracles we want that we fail to recognize the miracles God gives us. In our case we wanted Nick healed so badly that we prayed and prayed—and still pray—for that miracle. Yet over the years we've realized that God has performed many other miracles. Our son's amazing life has had many miraculous elements, from his role inspiring and leading others all around the world to God, to his marriage to Kanae and the births of their children. God has not healed Nick's body, but He has certainly blessed him and all of us who love him in many ways.

Being parents will surely challenge Nick and Kanae, and it will likely stress their bonds of marriage, but Dushka and I have great confidence that our son and his wife will continue to live a life without limits as they follow God's plan. Nick and Kanae may not be able to walk hand in hand or arm in arm, but they walk in faith together. Our experiences in raising Nick taught us that if you put your trust in God's way, He will provide you with all the strength you need.

TAKEAWAY THOUGHTS

- There is no shame in questioning why a child is burdened with disabilities, illness, or injuries. If we had no questions, we would not need faith in our lives. You may never understand why your child is afflicted, but you can be assured that it is not a punishment for you or the child. Your best option is to walk by faith, one step at a time, in the hope that you and your child will find purpose and meaning in your journey, as we have with Nick's.

- Acceptance of God's wisdom and love is one step. The next step is to put your faith into action and provide your child with a strong foundation of unconditional love, an unwavering sense of self-worth, and the knowledge that God does not make mistakes. He loves all His children equally.

- We are all imperfect because we are born into an imperfect world. God knows of our failings, and He knows we can all be healed by putting Him above earthly things. Romans 8:29 tells us, "For God knew his people in advance, and he chose them to become like his Son, so that his Son would be the firstborn among many brothers and sisters."

- No one expects parents to be grateful that their child has disabilities. Yet most of those I've known say they have experienced far more blessings and gratitude than they had ever imagined possible. Welcome the blessings and gratitude and focus on giving your child the best possible life.

- Don't dwell on the unknowns and your fears for your child's future. Ask God to love and protect your child. Surrender to Him control of the life He created while you focus on those things within your power.

- Feel free to pray for miracles for your child. I certainly pray for my son to be given arms and legs so that he can run with his children and hold them and his wife in his arms. I want that desperately for him. Yet when I see Nick with his wife and children, basking in the love they share, I no longer question God's plan for him. I marvel at it. I know it is for good and not for evil, and I thank Him for helping me become more compassionate and more understanding of what is truly important in this world.

Acknowledgments

This is my first book, and it has been a very emotional and enlightening experience. My son has written several books, and I have a new appreciation for all that goes into this process. I thank my wife, Dushka, for helping refresh and replenish my memories of raising Nick, as well as Aaron and Michelle. As always, Dushka provides a foundation of love, support and strength. I also thank all of our children for their input and support in this project, as well as for their constant and unconditional love.

Nick loaned me his writing partner, Wes Smith, for this project, and I appreciate all his hard work, patience, and persistence. Thanks also to those who helped bring this dream into reality: my literary agents, Jan Miller Rich and Nena Madonia at Dupree Miller and Associates, along with our publishing team at WaterBrook Multnomah, a division of Penguin Random House, which includes Tina Constable, Alex Field, Johanna Inwood, Bruce Nygren, and Laura Wright.

Most of all, I thank God: the Father, the Son Jesus Christ, and the Holy Spirit for blessing my life with so much love and for teaching me that every child is perfectly made.

Lastly, but no less important, thank you to all the people who pray for me, my wife, and ministry, and to those who financially support us. A big thank-you as well for helping us attain the goals of Life Without Limbs.

Bless all of you who read this book. I pray that my words open your hearts and minds in a fresh and dynamic way, moving you to put your faith into action while inspiring others to do the same.

Index

Let Nick Vujicic Inspire you to a Life Beyond Limits

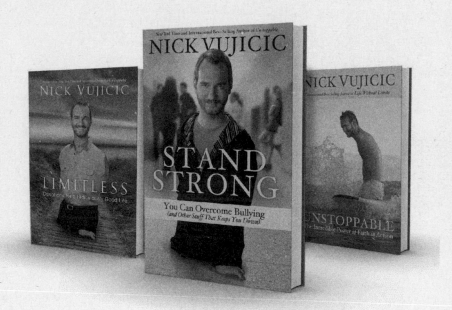

WATERBROOK PRESS

www.waterbrookmultnomah.com

What would your life be like if *anything* were possible?

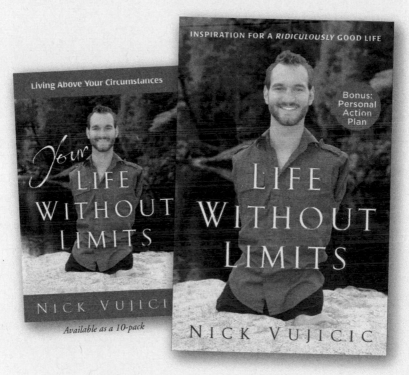

Nick tells the story of his physical disabilities and the emotional battle he endured while learning to deal with them as a child, teen, and young adult. Nick shares how his faith in God has been his major source of strength, and he explains that once he found a sense of purpose—inspiring others to better their lives and the world around them—he found the confidence to build a rewarding and productive life without limits. Let Nick inspire you to start living your own life without limits.

Read an excerpt from this book and more at
www.WaterBrookMultnomah.com!

IT DOESN'T TAKE A PERFECT PERSON TO FIND A PERFECT LOVE

In *Love Without Limits*, Nick and Kanae Vujicic tell how they improbably found each other, fell in love, and then fought to overcome skepticism from others about their relationship. Filled with practical advice for any couple, this inspiring book reminds us that love can overcome any obstacle when Christ is at the center of the relationship.

WATERBROOK PRESS

www.waterbrookmultnomah.com